New Brunswick
A Short History

Tim Frink

Stonington Books
Tim C. Frink
12 Winchester Road
Summerville, NB
E5S 1B7

Second Edition printed by Centennial Print, NB, 1999
First Edition printed by Centennial Print, NB, 1997

Canadian Cataloguing in Publication Data

Frink, Timothy.

New Brunswick A Short History

ISBN 0-9682500-1-7

1. New Brunswick — History.   I. Title

FC2461.F74 1997   971.5'1   C97-950161-X
F1043.F74 1997

Front Cover:
Artist unknown, American
The Great Fire at St. John, N.B., June 1877, 1877
hand-coloured lithograph on wove paper
20.5 x 32.1 cm (image)
Published by Currier & Ives, New York, 1877
*Courtesy: New Brunswick Museum, William B. Tennant
Collection, 21219*

Thanks to

Ardell Wills for the idea
Gillen for her patience and computer
Bruce and Gerry for adjusting my grammar
Shelly Rogers for saving my sanity
Regina Mantin and Peter Larocque and the staff at
    the NB Museum, Saint John
Brian and Dorothy Phelan
The staff at the Saint John Regional Library
The staff at the Provincial Archives, Fredericton
and all who helped with this book.

to my family

Contents

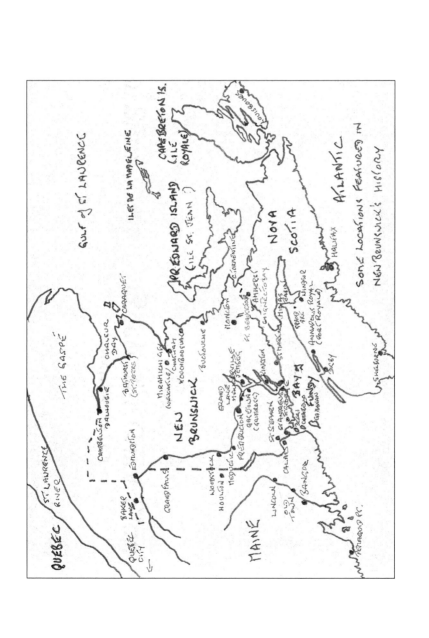

Some locations featured in
New Brunswick's history

Some Brief Notes on
New Brunswick A Short History

No part of the North American continent can boast a more violent, varied, or intriguing history than the 28,000 square miles (72,000 sq.km) that make up the land mass of present day New Brunswick. For one hundred and fifty years it marked the demarcation line and battleground between the Anglo-Saxons and the French as their age-old rivalry spilled over into the New World. During the Seventeenth Century it was the scene of a savage civil war between two factions of the French. Then after French power in the region had waned, and after the American Revolution, New Brunswick became the front line between the Anglo-Saxons who had rebelled against the Crown and those who had remained loyal.

In documenting the history for the area, it has to be noted that it was not until 1784 that New Brunswick became a political entity. Prior to that the region had a mind-addling array of designations, as it formed a part of other political units that grew or shrank across the map of the northeast coast of the continent; as the fortunes of war swept back and forth, or quills scratched out concessions in far distant capitals.

This story, insofar as is possible, has confined itself to the site that comprises the present day Province of New Brunswick, but strays at times into present day Nova Scotia, or the

State of Maine when it seems relevant or essential to do so. Since the multitude of political designations must be at least as confusing to the reader as it is to the writer it was thought that a chart might be helpful. To further confuse matters it will be noted that there were times that two names applied, depending on the point of view.

Named	By The English	By The French
Acadia	1604-1620	1604-1632
New England	1620-1621	
Nova Scotia (Alexandria)	1621-1632	
Acadia	1632-1654	1632-1667
Nova Scotia	1654-1667	
Acadia	1667-1691	
Massachusetts	1691-1696	
Nova Scotia	1696-1697	
Acadia	1697-1713	
New France		1713-1763
Nova Scotia (Sunbury Co)	1713-1784	
New Brunswick	1784-	

This brief history is not intended to be a scholarly work, but is meant to acquaint anyone interested, with some of the remarkable people and events that have shaped the province. Nor is it to be seen as some kind of public relations release, glossing over the darker happenings on one hand while hyping the more acceptable on the other. While 'political correctness' may take a beating once in a while, I have tried very hard to see both sides of every story — every story has them. I refer to it as objectivity, or at least objectivity the way I see it.

One

❦

The First Nations

When the first Europeans started straggling into Eastern North America, they came face to face with a population that had been living in the stone age, and overnight thrust them into the modern age. It was to be traumatic for both sides but moreso for the natives, or First Nations as they are now called. Originally the natives were all called Indians for no better reason than the first white explorers were looking for a short cut to India and made some wrong assumptions. Consequently, after generations being called Indians after someone else's mistake, some resentment has built up around the term.

The land mass that now comprises Eastern Maine, New Brunswick, the Gaspé Peninsula, Nova Scotia and Prince Edward Island was essentially occupied by two Algonquin tribes: the Mi'kmag and the Malicetes. They spoke a language that, while sharing the same roots, were not mutually comprehensible, rather like English and German today.

There were other differences between the two tribes. The Mi'kmag were oriented to a coastal life. They occupied the whole coastline from the Gaspé round the Chaleur Bay down to Chignecto, including all present day Nova Scotia and Prince Edward Island, and down the Fundy coast to Saint Martin's. This huge slice of present day New Brunswick included the drainage basins of the Restigouche, Miramichi and Petitcodiac river systems.

"That's not leaving much," you may say — not so. The Malicetes were left with a stranglehold on the Saint John River Valley and the Penobscot and St. Croix River systems and thereby controlled all the movement of supplies and news for this whole vast area. This was a fact quickly grasped by the French who stayed in as contenders for the possession of the Maritimes for one hundred and fifty years largely by maintaining good relations with them. The Malicetes were helped in this task by two sub groups of their tribe: the Passamaquoddies and the Penobscots who occupied the Fundy Islands and coastlands of Eastern Maine.

A third Algonquin group, the Abnaki, *People of the Dawn*, who inhabited the balance of Eastern Maine, also made alliances with the French, adding to the discomfort of the New Englanders and English settling in New Brunswick. In contrast to the Mi'kmaq and Malicetes who were nomads wandering from place to place wherever food or circumstances might dictate, the Abnakis lived in permanent settlements and grew corn.

All these tribal groupings of First Nations people lived together, for the most part, if not in complete harmony, at least in grudging acceptance of each other. Doubtless there were isolated clashes but generally turf rights seem to have been respected and there are no records of any major flare-ups. Major warfare was, in fact, foreign to these people's culture since tribal scale warfare calls for a formal political structure which they were able to do without. That is not to say, however, that inter-tribal violence did not exist and their highly organized Iroquoian neighbours, the Mohawks, were capable of war on a grand scale.

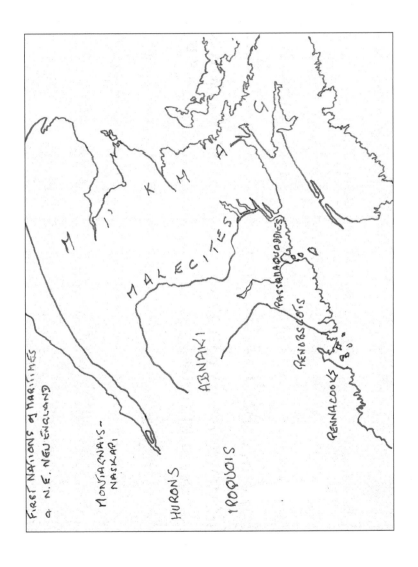

FIRST NATIONS of MARITIMES & N.E. NEW ENGLAND

MONTAGNAIS- NASKAPI

HURONS

IROQUOIS

ABNAKI

MALECITES

MIKMAKS

PASSAMAQUODDIES

PENOBSCOTS

PENNACOOKS

A clue to relations between Mi'kmag and Malecite can be found in their names for each other. Racial slurs involving dietary habits are not new. The Mi'kmag called the Malicetes 'Muskrats' and the Malicetes called the Mi'kmag 'Porcupines'.

Theories abound as to how the First Nations people arrived in the Americas in time to confuse the Europeans who thought that they had discovered a new route to India. Certainly they were there in plenty of time. Anthropologists show that they probably crossed from Asia by way of the Bering Strait at one of two periods of history. Evidence shows that between 50,000 B.C. and 8,000 B.C. there were two periods when a land bridge between Siberia and Alaska existed.

These land bridges occurred when advancing ice caps lowered sea levels to the point that the shallow Bering Strait was dry land. Evidence shows that an ice-free avenue down through central British Columbia could have provided a practical entryway for immigrants from Asia. It must be presumed that these migrants were fairly well advanced people because it takes a fair amount of talent to survive a northern Canadian climate under the best of circumstances. The fact that these people made that crossing and ultimately dispersed themselves throughout the continent tells us that they were already very capable people who were able to dress themselves in warm furs and build themselves weatherproof shelters. These were obviously skills they had before they made the crossing. Ice-free corridors through the southern Yukon and British Columbia would have led them southwards and eastwards until they had populated the continent.

This migration did not happen overnight. The first window between 50,000 B.C. and 40,000 B.C. was shorter but milder than the second window which occurred between 26,000 B.C. and 8,000 B.C., so migration could have taken place at either or both times. It is very clear, however, that it was not a mass migration. In the area which today comprises Canada and the United States there were at least a dozen separate linguistic groups; in other words, ethnic groups whose languages were as dissimilar as, say, Russian and French. Beyond that there were perhaps one hundred and fifty mutually unintelligible languages. These facts all tell us that the entry of First Nations people into North America came to pass over many, many years. When you add the even greater diversity of the linguistic groups in South America, the arguments for a long and protracted series of migrations are yet more compelling.

It was widely assumed by many settlers that since the natives appeared to look much the same (they don't) they must all come from the same common Asiatic root (they don't).

Comparing the North American natives with each other is superficially easy. They all tend to have an Asiatic look about them: the same general colouring, high cheekbones, dark slanted eyes — but look again, some tribes are short and squat; others are tall and lean. Some have wide Asian features while others have chiselled European features. Our First Nations people do not resemble the Chinese or Japanese whose numbers dominate present day Asia, but moreso the people on the periphery of those cultures — Indonesia, Central Asia and so on.

One young First Nations woman once argued with the writer, "Perhaps it all started here and some moved to Asia!" Well? Perhaps so!

An amazing fact about the Mi'kmag and Malecite people of the Maritimes is that despite the length of time they had inhabited the area, their numbers were remarkably low. It is generally conceded that in the early seventeenth century the native population of New Brunswick was a scant 2,000. This fact was reflected across the United States and Canada. Because of the great lapse in time between first contact and

European settling on the west coast, much guesswork has been used in arriving at a total — because by that time eastern populations had been decimated by war and disease. Nevertheless, few experts place that figure over six million.

The concept that the woods and plains were 'teeming with Indians' is clearly wrong, but why were the numbers so low? Longevity does not seem to have been any more of a problem for the First Nations people than it was for the whites. They lived to a ripe old age — eighties and nineties were common — until they became devastated by European contagions against which they had no genetic defences.

Perhaps they had already filled in their space to the point where their way of life could be maintained without degrading their environment. Their overnight shift from stone age to modern age would bring an end to that!

At this point, mention should be made of the Red Paint People who have been thought by some to be the forerunners of the natives first encountered by whites. Gravesites were discovered containing quantities of red ochre. Assumptions were made that the presence of this pigment held some special relevance to some primitive predecessors of the First Nations population. It was found, however, that the red ochre appeared in gravesites that post dated European landing and that the same mysterious presence of the pigment occurs in ancient sites throughout Europe and Asia. The ill-fated Beothuks of Newfoundland, moreover, painted themselves with red ochre causing Sebastian Cabot to call them red Indians — a name that stuck.

The generally nomadic existence of the Mi'kmag and Malicetes makes it difficult to get a complete picture of their lives before white settlement. Permanent settlements were few and far between, giving little opportunity for study by archaeologists, but enough information has been developed to give us some idea. The fact that they were able to survive in an extremely harsh climate tells us that they must have been an incredibly hardy and resourceful people in superb physical condition. They ate well.

The Mi'kmag, as might be expected from their coastal life, leaned more heavily upon seafood for their diets than did the Malicetes, but the latter still took full advantage of the salmon that poured into nearly all the rivers each spring. The woods ensured a steady supply of moose and deer — caribou at that time — not to mention porcupine and muskrat. Berries and wild greens would supplement their diets, sometimes corn and pumpkins if they stayed put long enough to grow them.

Cooking fish was often done by splitting it down the back and lashing it to a piece of wood where it would be half barbe-cued and half smoked before an open fire, still the best way to cook a salmon.

Meat would be roasted over the fire, held in place by a cleft stick and stews were popular, but painstakingly difficult to prepare. Water would have to be boiled by heating stones and dropping them into birchbark containers — a laborious process that must have made European cookware look really attractive to the cooks.

They fashioned their weapons and cutting tools out of flinty chert, jasper or various kinds of quartzes. They fashioned stone axes, adzes, gouges and chisels; with these tools they were able to make toboggans, snowshoes, birch bark boxes and wooden bowls. They found a bluish gray clay and from it made pottery and decorated it. They built sweat lodges to cleanse them-selves spiritually and physically. Above all, they built the birch bark canoe.

Canoe Making on St. Mary's Reserve, Fredericton c. 1905 *Courtesy: PANB #P5-381*

The birch bark canoe was an incredible tool and means of transport for New Brunswick with its unparalleled river systems. A properly built Malicete four-man canoe could be twenty feet in length, two feet across the beam and weigh under one hundred pounds, drawing only a few inches of water. By lightening up on the load the draught could be reduced to a mere two to three inches.

The significance of these facts is that even the most inconspicuous streams could become a part of their travel plans, enabling them to switch from one river system to another. There is probably nowhere on earth where a comparable area is served so well by its rivers. The St. John, the Restigouche, the Nepisquit, the Miramichi, the Petitcodiac and St. Croix make every corner of the province accessible by canoe. Portages throughout this area hardly ever exceed twelve miles, more than enough, you might say, when carrying canoe, paddles, supplies and whatever other business on the back, but chicken-feed for a Malicete warrior.

The fact that the rivers made such good avenues of communication resulted in an almost complete absence of roads or even trails in New Brunswick until the time of the Loyalist influx towards the end of the eighteenth century. In early days the only trails were the portage routes from one waterway to another. Nevertheless, transport of supplies or information from the north shore to the Penobscot in the west, for example, could be carried out with incredible speed and without being exposed to the hazards of the open sea. Even the coastal region from Shediac to the Miramichi was largely protected by a system of sandbars, islands and lagoons along the coast.

Central to all of these systems was the St. John River itself which was not only the pivotal river in all the various systems; it became the line of communication between the St. Lawrence Valley and Nova Scotia. To give some idea of how

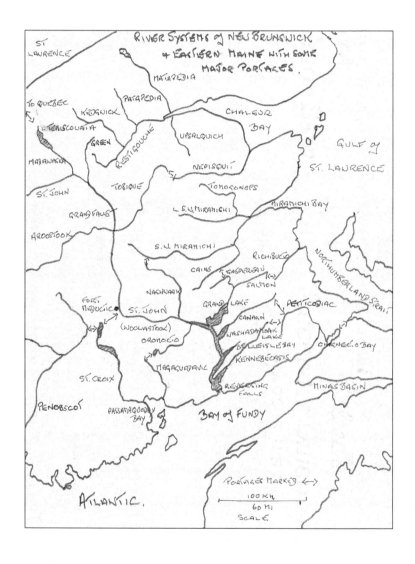

efficient the Malicete rivermen were, one run was recorded from Chignecto, on the New Brunswick/Nova Scotia border to Quebec city, a distance of 700 kilometres (400 miles), in seven days! Upstream!

One can only imagine the physical conditioning of these men who could paddle against the river current all day and pole their little craft up roaring rapids, carrying their loads over portages day after day.

The 'predam' St. John River had only one natural obstacle — the seventy-five foot drop at Grand Falls. A legend persists.

Perhaps an historical account is no place for a legend but this legend is persistent enough to have us believe it might well be grounded in fact. Legend and history have a way of becoming fairly interchangeable at times, so it is offered without apology.

It is said that the Malicetes had a longstanding struggle with the warlike Mohawks, an Iroquoian tribe, part of the five nations confederation to the west. Repeated encroachments had taken place and in one such encroachment into Malicete territory, five hundred Mohawk warriors had arrived at the Madawaska and captured a Malicete hunter and his family.

The Mohawks killed all but the wife of the hunter, who was kept as a guide to lead the war party to the main Malicete village at Meductic. An attack of this scale would have been devastating to her people.

The war party with their unwilling captive moved swiftly down the river that Malicetes called Woolastook, the "good river." When they came to the long calm stretch of water above the falls, the woman told her captors that the quiet waters led to her tribal valley. Many of the warriors took their paddles out of the water, letting the canoes run in the current with only a steersman to control the craft.

When the roar of the falls reached them she calmed the fears of the steersmen by telling them that the sound came from a tributary. By the time they realized they had been tricked it was too late and the entire force was swept over the falls and destroyed. In a happier version the young widow dives to safety at the last moment.

Not legend, but factual, is the story about the remarkable Mi'kmag chief Membertou who, it is said, met Jacques Cartier when he made landfall on New Brunswick's North Shore and was still going strong when he met DesMonts at Port Royal some seventy years later.

When his tribesmen, who had been guiding the DesMonts/ Champlain exploration of the coast, brought back Chief Pennoniac's body, Membertou was outraged to hear that he had been killed by the Armouchiquois tribe.

Vowing revenge, the aged chief led a party of warriors across the treacherous forty mile expanse of the Bay of Fundy, to the St. John River where he enlisted the aid of the local Malicetes. At the head of five hundred warriors, he struck out for Saco, south of present day Portland, Maine, a two hundred and fifty mile (400 km.) run.

At Saco, Membertou caught up with the Armouchiquois chief Bessaber and slew him. Honour satisfied, he returned to Port Royal.

Over the years, writings have made much of the cruelty and savagery of the First Nations people and since all of the histories were written by the whites or their descendants, there was not much argument raised against the concept. It must be

The falls at Grand Falls taken from the bridge   *Courtesy: PANB #P9/3*

presumed that the natives were pretty hard on their captives. They led a hard life themselves and had their own cultural attitudes towards captives. For one thing, the use of captured foes as slaves was commonplace. The treatment of these slaves, as always, depended very much upon who the master was. For the most part, torture of prisoners seemed to have taken the form of unpleasant baiting or indifference to the suffering of others. It is probably fair to say that being a prisoner of the French or the English was not much fun either.

We gain some insight into life as a captive from the memoirs of John Gyles, a twelve-year-old New England boy from Pemaquid, Maine, who was captured by Malicetes in a raid on that settlement in 1689 and brought to Fort Meductic. He was treated kindly by his master but abused by others in the tribe. This remarkable boy survived for six years among the Malicetes before being sold to a French trader who ultimately gave him his freedom, but all this is another story.

While with the Malicetes, he was sent together with another boy to fetch the meat of a moose which had been killed at some distance from the fort. It was bitterly cold and once they had reached the carcass, John lit a fire which warmed him and melted his frozen clothing and the falling snow as it lighted on him. It was a mistake, common enough among inexperienced woods travellers and often a fatal one. Soaking wet from sweat and melted snow, his clothing re-froze immediately he left the warmth of the fire and his moccasins clad his feet like blocks of ice.

All day he slogged along in the tracks of the Malicete, not stopping for food or warmth, knowing that if he did stop he would never get up again. When he staggered into the wigwam, the Malicetes cut his clothes off and peeled the clouts off his feet which swelled and turned black.

As circulation returned painfully to his feet, the Malicetes told him comfortingly that he was probably going to die. Nonetheless, they treated his feet with a balsam salve. In no time he was wobbling along on his heels with the help of a staff. Fortunately, the band had enough food that they could stay put for a few days. According to Gyles' memoirs, by the time they were ready to move on they were able to rig him up with:

> two little hoops, something in the form of a snowshoe; and sewing them to my feet, I was able to follow them in their tracks, on my heels, from place to place, though sometimes half leg deep in snow and water, which gave me the most acute pain imaginable; but I must walk or die.[1]

The First Nations of New Brunswick and Nova Scotia came into contact with the French first and always had more empathy with them than they did with the English. There were practical considerations. The French never showed themselves to be as dedicated to settling as the English and their numbers were not nearly as great. They felt much less threatened by the French.

The French immediately recognized the Malicetes' role in the vital link between Quebec and its colonies in Acadia and by astute use of the church and its missionaries were able to maintain a strong alliance with them until they themselves ceased to be a power in the area. For decades, a handful of French colonists and missionaries were able to keep the ever-increasing numbers of English settlers off balance by clever use of their native allies.

New Brunswick came close to being plunged into the actual theatre of the revolutionary war in 1778, thanks to the Malicetes and their Passamaquoddy and Penobscot sub tribes. As always in times of war the First Nations came to be very much in demand as allies, and George Washington was successful in enlisting six hundred of them to his cause. Immediately, life became very difficult for English or American settlers living in the St. John River Valley, as they became threatened by the rebellious Natives.

Chief Tomah on his way downriver at the head of ninety canoes, sent ahead what amounted to a declaration of war. The immediate future of Saint John looked bleak as it lay virtually defenseless in the path of the invasion. The future of New Brunswick suddenly lay in the hands of James White, one of the original merchants of Saint John, who doubled as deputy superintendent of the community.

White set out single-handed to meet chief Tomah and his flotilla and had no trouble locating them in Long Reach, a few miles upriver. The Malicetes and their allies impressed by the man's courage stopped and listened to what he had to say. Chief Tomah told everyone to wait while he communicated with the great spirit and listened to what he had to say. He lay face down in the sand for nearly an hour while everyone stood around shifting their weight from one foot to the other. Eventually the chief stirred himself and announced that the great spirit wished him to remain on good terms with King George. There was further discussion and then they all moved on to Fort Howe where White now had backup from Major Studholme, the Garrison commander, and Michael Francklin, Superintendent of Indian Affairs from Halifax. In no time agreements were made, gifts exchanged hands — the crisis had passed.

There was another critical coin flip on the Miramichi, where the Mi'kmag were being elbowed aside by Scottish settlers. Still sentimentally attached to the French who were backing the Americans, the Mi'kmag started making trouble in 1775, stealing cattle and burning buildings. By 1777, things had gotten so uncomfortable that most of the Scots under William Davidson and John Cort were forced to take temporary refuge at Maugerville.

Some of the Scottish families, however, elected to stay. The Stewarts, Gillies and Martins had developed a trust between themselves, and some of the local Natives including the Julian family who took the Scots under their wing and offered them protection from the surrounding turmoil.

Eventually, *H.M.S. Viper* was sent to the river to straighten things out. Flying the French colours and sending a longboat ashore under the American flag, they enticed the unsuspecting Mi'kmag to the riverbank and jumped them, taking sixteen of them captive and putting them aboard in chains.

Caiffe, the Mi'kmag chief who had been doing all the rabble rousing, was able to escape and was declared a rebel, while the rest were told to go home and behave themselves. John Julian was recognized as "Chief of the Miramichi Indians" and on July 20, 1779, a treaty of peace was signed between him and Captain Harvey of the *Viper*. Shortly afterwards the *Viper* sailed for Quebec City along with the sixteen hostages.

Naturally Chief John's first concern was for the welfare of these hostages. Were they to be freed? If not what was going to be done with them? Who was supposed to pay for the support of their families? With this question in mind he enlisted the aid of his brother and a few other senior tribesmen and went to Halifax where he met with Michael Francklin, Superintendent of Indian Affairs.

Francklin having already dealt with the First Nations threat against Saint John must have found the Julians easy to deal with. First he would not even discuss the sixteen hostages until the delegation had signed a treaty.

By this treaty the Julians ended up taking responsibility for the recent uprising in that they had not done enough to discourage it. Furthermore they undertook to protect the rights and property of British subjects in future. In return gifts changed hands and Francklin assured them that their rights would be protected and that all their needs would be met by traders — in exchange for furs. The hostages remained where they were until Governor Haldimand in Quebec shipped them all back to Halifax where they were greeted without much enthusiasm. Sixteen warriors took up more confinement space than the authorities could comfortably afford, so they released fourteen of them, retaining only two ring leaders.

In 1787 John Julian concluded another treaty with Governor Parr's regime in Halifax. For years prior to the Revolutionary War the Mi'kmag had been promised land grants by various administrations but nothing had ever been finalized. Now finally there was recognition of their loyalty and a grant of 20,000 acres (8,000 ha.) stretching both sides of the Northwest Miramichi from the Mouth of the Southwest branch past the mouth of the Sevogle River. It was too good to last. Davidson and the others who had left during the uprising returned and reclaimed their original grants. The First Nations whose sense of property rights was already, to say the least, confused, were thunderstruck to find that in some important areas Governor Parr had generously given them lands that he had already given to someone else.

The whittling process had started. Now loyalists started flooding in from the American colonies putting more pressure on the Native bands — not just the Mi'kmag bands of the Miramichi but all over what was now New Brunswick. From this point on the First Nations people were no longer considered a threat or even a force to be reckoned with. It was the beginning of a long dark time for them before they would band together again to demand their rights.

The First Nations

It was in the 1960's that the First Nations of New Brunswick started to aggressively pursue their native rights as laid out in various treaties dating back over the preceding centuries. Most revolved around hunting and fishing rights, until the summer of 1998, when a court confirmed that the natives held cutting rights on crown lands. This bit of news sent a lot of very senior legislators, and forest products company executives, running for their legal counsel, while native logging crews took to the woods in force, until the decision was reversed by a superior court.

Two

༄

The First Settlers —
The French

Perhaps the very first Europeans to visit our shores were the Vikings. Some claim to recognize the Island of Grand Manan in their ancient writings. We know that they reached Newfoundland and it is easy to believe that those great adventurers might have taken that one extra step. We just do not know.

We are fairly certain, however, that long before the first formal settlements at the dawn of the seventeenth century, our shores were frequently visited by European fishermen, English, Basque, Breton and Portugese. For a time they kept the whereabouts of their new 'fishing hole' a closely guarded secret; but there is no evidence that any settled here. At most, it seems, they set up seasonal camps as bases for their fishing operations.

In 1534, Jacques Cartier sailed down to New Brunswick's north shore and named the Baie Chaleur, after its warm waters, but despite this early start, colonization moved at a snail's pace. It was not until 1607 that Samuel de Champlain sailed into the Miramichi. Then, in the following year under the leadership of DesMonts, he sailed into Fundy Bay, coasting up the south shore to Minas Basin, past Chignecto Point to present day New Brunswick.

In his capacity as Royal Geographer, Champlain kept careful notes from which one can recognize such features as the St. Martins area, an iron ore deposit east of Cape Spencer, the mouth of the St. John River, the St. Croix and Grand Manan Island.

The DesMonts expedition was commissioned by Henry IV of France to 'settle La Cadie' and picked out a small island near the mouth of the St. Croix River that would be easy to defend. They called it St. Croix Island.

The experiment was a disaster. Few of the settlers survived the winter of 1604-1605. Scurvy, that mysterious killer of early adventurers, was to blame for most of the deaths. Out of a total number of eighty-seven, fifty-one survived; and only eleven were unaffected. An account of 1608 describes the progress of the disgusting disease:

> First their legs became thick and swollen, the muscles shrunken and black; then the disease crept up to the hips, thighs and shoulders to the arms and neck; their mouths became so charged with rotten flesh which spread all over and grew afresh between night and morning....

If they had but known that they were being killed by a dietary deficiency, the cures lay all about them. They might have wondered why the Passamaquoddies were unaffected and used their dietary supplement, a spruce beer.

In fact, their choice of an island location was their biggest problem. Water had to be rowed over from the mainland and their gardens withered. They also probably planted too late in a climate where only ninety frost-free days can be counted on. That year, the snow started on October sixth. The little outpost of the French empire used up all of the available wood and were unable to get any from the mainland because of

21

MAP of PASSAMAQUODDY BAY SHOWING FRENCH SETTLEMENTS & INDIAN CAMPS.

dangerous ice conditions in the river. They shivered and thirsted and suffered, praying for delivery from the hell they found themselves in.

St. Croix Island later became known as Bone Island.

No further attempts to settle the Passamaquoddy Bay area were made until the Sieur St. Aubin was granted a seigniory in 1684; but even then the colony was never more than a small group of fishermen and traders centred round the islands and what are now St. Stephen and St. Andrews. The French settlement there ceased to exist completely after Benjamin Church's punitive raid from Massachusetts in 1704.

A word should be written about the operation of the French Seignorial system, because it explains many of the shortcomings of their attempts to settle and colonize Acadia. A seignorial grant from the French king gave the Seigneur, forever title to his lands, fishing and hunting rights, trading and the administration of justice to his tenants. With all this came responsibilities. The Seigneur was to settle colonists on his lands in stated numbers and at stated time periods. He had to keep the rivers open for navigation and build roads.

Other small settlements sprang up on Caton's Island at the head of Long Reach in the St. John River, and Fort Jemseg, a bit further up stream. There was activity at the mouth of the river also.

At first, in practice, the seigniories were granted by the Company of New France, acting on the King's behalf, then by the company of the West Indies. When all *their* rights reverted to the King in 1674 his representatives in Quebec City made the awards subject to his later approval.

The first two seigniories in New Brunswick were granted to the Governor of Acadia De Razilly at St. Croix and La Tour at Saint John, both in 1635. The following year Nicholas Denys received a grant on the North Shore at St. Peter's, now Bathurst. Eventually thirty-five would be granted, but by the early 1700s all had vanished. Why?

The experiences of two of these three men go a long way to answering that question, but the system had inherent weaknesses. At first glance the system in itself seems sound; large parcels of land would be put out for development and in no time the whole area would be opened up by a group of thriving communities.

The system worked to a certain degree in Quebec though it probably retarded development there in the long run too. In Acadia, however, conflicting ambitions and lack of success in attracting colonists all contributed to its downfall. Their owners often looked upon their rights as a license to exploit. Targets were not met and by 1703 most were in default and revoked by the Crown.

There is usually an exception to prove the rule and here is no exception. The Seigniory of La Vallières at the head of the Bay of Fundy was highly successful and featured the type of development that the Acadians had a great gift for: the reclaiming of marshland. Many of them must have come from parts of France where this type of land reclamation had been well known. Certainly when they saw the huge expanses of marshlands caused by the fifty foot (15 m.) rise and fall of Fundy tides, they knew exactly what to do.

The New Englanders may have scoffed at the Acadians' apparent reluctance to clear forest land, but they worked hard enough. They would fill in low spots by sinking six rows of upright trees and filling them with more trees laid horizontally; they then packed them with clay. Fresh water was allowed to escape by leaving openings where necessary and fitting them with valves called 'aboiteaux' which not only let the fresh water out but prevented the salt water from coming in.

A great amount of very rich land was quickly made into useful farming country. It also concentrated a major proportion of the Acadian population into a relatively small area.

The lives of the three original seigneurs were not long becoming intermeshed. Their world was, after all, a small one in many respects.

Working out of his base at St. Peters (Bathurst) and using DeRazilly shipping, Nicholas Denys opened up a thriving lumber trade and his future seemed to be assured. When Governor DeRazilly died he was succeeded by a seigneur from Port Royal by the name of Charles d'Aulnay de Charnisay. D'Aulnay had one consuming ambition which was total control of all Acadia; and everywhere he cast his eye, he saw potential threats to his power. One of these threats was Nicholas Denys, so wielding his power as Governor, d'Aulnay put a stop to his trade and reduced him to ruin; even in death d'Aulnay would come back to haunt him through his widow who had Denys arrested and clapped into a Quebec jail.

After his release, he returned once more to St. Peters where he was again thrown into jail by d'Aulnay's successor and his business burned. This time, when he was released, he took no chances and obtained a commission from King Louis of France and set up once more, this time in Cape Breton. Apparently neither the change of venue nor the king's signature were enough to save this unfortunate man and once more his business was burned to the ground.

Home in France, Denys tried to make a living writing about the country that he obviously loved so much, but still financial success eluded him. He returned once more to Bathurst where he died an old man — not rich — but clearly where he wanted to be. Success did come to Nicholas Denys posthumously, for his writings became required reading for anyone studying life on the North Atlantic seaboard in the seventeenth century.

One of the other seignioral grantees at that time was, as we have seen, Charles de Saint Etienne de La Tour. La Tour's name belies his origins — his father, a shameless social climber, had been a master mason in Paris, and it is very likely that his son's determined character had much to do with his will to survive. In seventeenth century France, to be born outside of the aristocracy made any kind of advancement very difficult. His origins also go far to explain why the highborn d'Aulnay always came out on top in their confrontations at court.

La Tour drew a grant that included the mouth of the St. John river, which led to the most extraordinary story in New Brunswick history. The very improbability of the people involved and the sequence of events must give rise to doubts, but in essence the story is true, and gives us a helpful insight as to how the general lack of cohesion among the French hindered their attempts to create a North American empire. Once more without apology.

In the eyes of King James I of England, the entire area of the Eastern Maine, New Brunswick, and Nova Scotian peninsula was 'Nova Scotia'. In 1621 he bestowed this huge tract of land upon a Sir William Alexander who modestly renamed the land north of the bay of Fundy, Alexandria. No doubt to make himself feel even more at home, he renamed the St. John River the *Clyde*. Thankfully neither name stuck.

King James also granted two baronetcies to Charles de la Tour's father Claude who was one of Sir William's grantees, and Claude was allowed to pass one on to his son, which explains to a great extent why Charles had something approaching a special relationship with the English. It also explains why Francoise is often referred to as Lady La Tour. Apart from the times Charles was buttering up his potential allies in New England, he seldom if ever used his title, but worked hard to obtain a commission and a grant from Louis XIII. In 1635, the company of New France formally granted La Tour the seigniory that included the fort and habitation at the mouth of the St. John river. He held, at this point, nominal control of the 'Nova Scotia' part of Acadia with the exception of the settlement and fort at Port Royal which belonged to d'Aulnay. La Tour, by virtue of his position at the site of present day Saint John, held practical control over the trading with the Indians of the Maine/New Brunswick area, which nominally belonged to d'Aulnay. We have already seen d'Aulnay's burning ambition to control all of Acadia and if Denys was thought to be a threat to that end, La Tour must be doubly so. It was a clear cut case of virtue and goodness against the evils of greed and ambition, well perhaps not quite, but the stage was set with each man occupying a stronghold in the midst of the other's lands.

Charles de La Tour was a Huguenot (French Protestant) by birth but at this stage had turned Catholic — perhaps to improve his relations with the French court. His wife, Francoise Marie Jacquelin, was the daughter of a physician from Nogent le Rotrol, a small town halfway between Chartres and Le Mans. She was a devout Huguenot and remained so for the rest of her life. Nevertheless, despite the high feelings that tended to go hand in hand with religion there was no discord in the La Tour household on that account.

Together they lived in style in their 180 foot square (54 m. sq.) fort at the mouth of the St. John River. They had a retinue of retainers and soldiers for their security; trade with the Indians was brisk. They dealt with tribesmen all the way up the river valley and well down into present day Maine. Life was treating the La Tours kindly. It was too good to last.

Of the two rivals, d'Aulnay was better connected at the French court, having the ear of the all powerful Cardinal Richelieu, controller of the royal council. He brought charges against La Tour for a variety of crimes, even treason, on the grounds that he was hiring English soldiers, and in 1641 La Tour was summoned to France to answer the accusation.

Calculating his chances for a fair hearing in Paris to be slim, La Tour wisely ignored the summons, and while d'Aulnay returned to France to plead his treason case, sturdied up his fort and sent urgent requests for help to Governor Winthrop in Boston. In seeking support from New England, La Tour was fighting an uphill battle. Governor Winthrop may have been sympathetic to his cause but New England was unflinchingly English and Protestant. Widespread support for a French Catholic was not to be forthcoming. La Tour's envoys were treated with respect but no practical aid was given. D'Aulnay, by now, was back in Acadia and thought it worthwhile to send a copy of the arrest warrant to Winthrop. He also blockaded the St. John River with a force of five ships and five hundred men, but not before La Tour had managed to get some help from La Rochelle, the Huguenot port/stronghold on the Bay of Biscay, and was able to add another one hundred and forty men to his command.

In the middle of June, 1643, the citizens of Boston were startled out of their wits by the sight of a French ship sailing up the harbour, firing its guns. It was soon clear, however, that they were not under attack; it was just La Tour back looking for help and firing a salute. Charles and Francoise La Tour slipping through d'Aulnay's blockade, perhaps in one of Fundy's famous fogs, had chanced upon the ship *Clement*, out of La Rochelle which had taken them on to Boston.

Once again, Governor Winthrop wanted to help La Tour, but religious intolerance was one of the guiding forces of New England politics at the time and for some time after. Once again he could offer little more than his best wishes. La Tour was able to do a little better on his own account making enough friends to gather a hundred men and four ships to his cause, with which he sailed bravely off for Saint John.

D'Aulnay was still sailing back and forth confident in the belief that he still had the couple bottled up in their fort. We can only imagine his reaction when he saw them sailing cheerfully up the bay. He reacted by hauling up all the canvas he could find and making a beeline for Port Royal with the La Tours in hot pursuit.

La Tour followed him right into his stronghold where he killed a few people and made off with a shipload of skins making the trip worthwhile.

Once more d'Aulnay, infuriated by the apparent impossibility of ridding himself of these two pests, took himself off to Paris to press his charges. Unknown to him, Francoise La Tour, was at the same time, drumming up support in the Huguenot stronghold of La Rochelle. D'Aulnay got wind of her presence there and was able to get a warrant for her arrest on grounds of treason, but Francoise was warned of her impending arrest and made good her escape to England, where she managed to get a ship with a cargo of ammunition and provisions for her husband.

For months, La Tour waited anxiously and finally turned once more to Boston for help. He was not able to come up with anything much as usual, some supplies but no real help. His ship had barely cleared Boston Harbour when Francoise showed up there with her London ship and a strong urge to kill her captain, a well known reprobate by the name of Jean Bailly.

The captain had been having second thoughts about his commission since running into d'Aulnay's ship just south of Cape Sable. He had been boarded and it had been necessary to hide Francoise La Tour and her attendants in one of the holds. Naturally, he was nervous about meeting d'Aulnay again and decided that a little trading with the natives up and down the coast was a better idea than sailing up the Bay to Saint John. When he finally berthed in Boston, Francoise promptly and successfully sued the captain for £2,000 which she used to transfer her cargo to other ships. Finally, after a year's absence she headed for home; Charles must have been glad to see her.

D'Aulnay, furious to find that he had been outmaneuvered once more by this remarkable woman and stung by Boston's complicity, captured a New England boat that was trying to reach the La Tours with food and munitions. He then turned the crew out onto Partridge Island, outside Saint John, in the middle of winter, and left them to their own devices. Finally, he provided them with a leaky shallop and somehow they made it back to Boston. He then set about planning his final act of revenge. It was April 1645.

One might wonder if Charles La Tour had any other reason for his endless and fruitless trips to Boston. Nevertheless, April finds him pinned down there once more by d'Aulnay's blockade while Françoise held the fort with dwindling supplies of powder and other provisions.

One day spirits soared in the fort as a sail was seen working its way up the Bay. Excitement filled the air at the expected return of La Tour. The Bay became obscured by fog for awhile and when it next lifted, the ship was right at their door — and opened fire.

Francoise could easily have taken refuge with the local Malicetes, who were friendly, and abandoned the fort. Her own soldiers wanted to take down the flag and surrender, but she was made of sterner stuff. She refused to leave the fort and shamed her soldiers into fighting back. They killed some sailors and did some damage to the ship which pulled off. The garrison waited all night, but at dawn, a native came to report that the ship had left shortly after sunset.

A few days later, another sail was seen approaching through the mists. This time, the attack was more determined. The raiders overcame the sentries and were at the gates of the fort, but Francoise led her soldiers and fought off the first charge. She was now out of powder.

Unaware of Francoise's vulnerability, d'Aulnay offered the garrison clemency if they would surrender. Realizing the hopelessness of her situation and hoping to save the lives of her troops, she consented.

D'Aulnay, true to form, was not a gracious victor and made Francoise La Tour stand with a rope around her neck and watch as he hanged her garrison one by one in front of her. They were not hanged by the quick and merciful 'drop', but by strangulation. Her own life was spared as was that of her son Charles, but she died shortly after and was buried by the river that had become her turbulent home. D'Aulnay after a decade of feuding was now undisputed Lord of all Acadia. He did not live to enjoy his office long, drowning in a boating accident near Port Royal, under the interested gaze of a Mi'kmag he had beaten a few days earlier. It was 1650.

When Charles La Tour heard of his enemy's death, he had been living in semi-exile among the natives of Eastern Canada. Now he sailed for France, obtained a pardon from His Majesty and had himself appointed d'Aulnay's successor, perhaps the same who threw Nicholas Denys into jail. There is an inconsistency here, since by other accounts La Tour and Denys were always good friends with d'Aulnay as the common enemy.

Just to tidy up any loose ends, Charles La Tour married d'Aulnay's widow, Jeanne Motin. They lived together, happily as far as we know until his death in 1666.

When you consider that political control of New Brunswick had changed about nine times by the time of confederation, it is easy to understand why so many of the settlements were either short-lived or changed hands so often that the occupants barely bothered to unpack their bags. Political control actually changed six times between 1654 and 1697 among the English, New Englanders and French — it even came under Dutch rule for four years!

The turmoil created by the war between D'Aulnay and La Tour set the scene for the next hundred years as settlers tried desperately to live their lives in something approaching normalcy. Even now, apart from the thriving Acadian communities around the Tantramar marshes, settlements were essentially trading posts, few and far between. One such was Fort Jemseg on the Jemseg River, a short stretch of water between the St. John River and Grand Lake, a pivotal location for trade running up and down the St. John Valley and all the land to the east.

A trading post had originally been established there by New Englanders under Thomas Temple, but he was forced to hand it over to De Joibert, when the country was ceded back to the French. De Joibert repaired the fort and strengthened it, but in 1674 both he and the fort were captured by a Dutch frigate captain named Jurriaen Aernouts.

Captain Aernouts is hard to explain in any meaningful way. He claimed to have a commission from the Dutch Governor of Curacao to "plunder and despoil all the enemies of Holland," which gave him lots of scope, but before he was able to bring action against any English colonies, the Dutch made peace with England. At loose ends he teamed up with a John Rhoade who knew where the French trading posts were.

Aernouts and Rhoade captured De Joibert and his family at Jemseg and removed them to Boston where they held them for ransom for one thousand beaver pelts. They held the unfortunate De Joiberts in Boston while Count Frontenac, the Governor of New France in Quebec, sent bills of exchange to La Rochelle. It was not until the Boston authorities cashed the bills that the De Joiberts won their freedom, and they returned to Jemseg. Eventually the post passed on to Louis d'Amour and his wife Marguerite.

Peace reigned at Jemseg for some years after that. In 1695 the D'Amours bought a young English lad from a Malicete; his name was John Gyles. They treated the boy with kindness and he worked willingly for them in the trading post where he was soon trusted with the keys. The following year, an expedition from New England under the command of Colonel Hawthorne and Benjamin Church came up the river destroying every French settlement they could find.

Hearing of the destruction heading their way John Gyles's new owners asked him to leave a note on the trading post door requesting that the d'Amours property be spared because of the kindness they had shown to him. They then all took refuge on Grand Lake while old Ben Church went storming up the valley, killing and burning as he went. They returned when it was safe to find that far from facing ruin their property was untouched.

Marguerite d'Amour deserved to have her property spared; she is known to have ransomed at least three other English captives from the Malicetes, a girl and two men. Church's expedition got no further than Fort Nashwaak where he met spirited resistance from Joseph De Villebon who had, in fact, been responsible for organizing many of the Indian raids that Church was avenging. The old warrior for once let discretion overrule valour and retired gracefully downriver.

The d'Amours, good people that they were, wanted to adopt John and give him a home; he preferred, however, to return to his own people and they respected his wishes.

Gyles' story was not all misery and hardship; he managed to keep a sense of humour. He tells a story about a field of wheat that was being decimated by a flock of grackles. The local priest was called in to solve the problem, all other remedies having failed. The Jesuit came to banish the noisy and hungry pests with 'a basin of holy water and a staff with a little brush'. He paraded up and down the field along with a retinue of about thirty people, scattering holy water and grackles before him, but the birds, unimpressed, quickly settled back into the ripe grain behind them. Viewing his lack of success in ravishing the grackles with all the equanimity in the world he blamed it upon the sinfulness of the congregation. He was not one to come up short on faith. Gyles writes:

> the same friar has vainly attempted to banish the mosquitoes from Signecto [Chignecto?] but the sins of the people there were also too great for him to prevail, but, on the other hand, it seemed that more came, a fact which caused the people to suspect that some had come for the sins of the Jesuit also.[1]

Three

✤

Boundaries

The attitudes of both great colonial powers towards their possessions in North America were generally marked by a deep and impenetrable stupidity. Huge tracts of land would be traded back and forth without a thought given to those who were trying to make them work. Europe-sized pieces of land would be given to Royal favourites who only had the slightest idea of where they were or what they represented. The European mind has never been able to come to grips with the vast spaces of North America and as a consequence, it was centuries before any meaningful boundaries took shape in the northern part of British North America.

It should be noted that this was not true of the colonies of New England. The New Englanders arrived as protesters looking for a new kind of society and had no time for the highly stratified society of the Mother Country. Self-reliance was all important to them; they wanted no troops from England on their soil and their governors were chosen from among their own, as were their governing bodies. Consequently there was never any question as to where their colonial boundaries lay — except between Maine and New Brunswick, and Maine and Quebec.

The Treaty of Ryswick signed by the Kings of England, France, Spain and the Holy Roman Emperor donated virtually all of the gigantic Hudson's Bay area to the French and allowed them to retain possession of Acadia. The French selected the Kennebec River as the border, while the New Englanders held that it was at the St. Croix. There was still very little Acadian settlement outside of the marshlands, but they did maintain a tight working relationship with the Micmacs, Malicetes and another kindred tribe to their immediate west, the Abnakis. Egged on by the French missionaries, raids on English settlements at the extremes of their range had become commonplace. It had been such a raid that had brought the young John Gyles to Fort Meductic.

In 1703, the Governments of Massachusetts and New Hampshire went a long way to polarizing native sentiment by offering £20 for any Indian prisoner under ten and £40 for an older prisoner — or his scalp! This type of low grade guerilla warfare culminated in February 1704 when a French/Indian force struck down into the upper Connecticut valley and fell upon Deerfield which still suffered from the memory of 'King' Philip's uprising in 1675-1676 when an alliance of Massachusetts and Connecticut tribes, made a belated attempt to stem the relentless advance of the whites. This time thirty-eight settlers were killed in the raid; one hundred and six prisoners were taken. Nineteen more were killed on the brutal two hundred and fifty mile (400 km.) march through the snows to Montreal. By the time the prisoners were finally released two years later only sixty-four lived to see Boston again.

In May 1704, Ben Church once more gathered a force for a punitive expedition to Acadia. With six hundred men, including a number of friendly natives aboard three warships, fourteen transports, and with thirty-six whaling boats for landing craft, they headed northeast. They attacked Pentagoet, taking several prisoners, destroyed any sign of French settlement at Passamaquoddy and sailed on up Fundy Bay to Minas Basin. The Acadian settlers, about three hundred of them in all, fled for the woods. The New Englanders took some pleasure in burning their buildings and seizing their supplies. Fifty houses were burned to the ground and a number of cattle killed. They also breached the Acadian dykes, allowing the sea to flood the marshlands.

By the Treaty of Utrecht in 1713, Acadia was once more handed back to the English, but the two sides had predictably varying concepts of what Acadia actually consisted of. The English presumed it to be present day New Brunswick and Nova Scotia while the French, for the purposes of this exercise, considered that Nova Scotia was enough to lose, and denied that the transfer included New Brunswick.

Although the whole area now came under English rule there was little immigration from New England. The Acadians continued to dominate everyday life, and it is probably fair to say that, although attempts were made to secure oaths of allegiance from the Acadians to the English Crown, they were left pretty much to their own devices.

View of Miramichi, a French Settlement in the Gulf of St. Lawrence, Destroyed by Brigadier Murray Detached by General Wolfe for That Purpose, From the Bay of Gaspe, 1760

Courtesy: NBM #40455

Four

The Expulsion of the Acadians

The oath of Allegiance was to become a thorny problem which would eventually result in one of the most appalling acts ever committed in the name of the English Crown.

Two separate images emerge of the Acadian people in the first half of the eighteenth century, probably neither of them quite accurate. The Acadian population base was still heavily concentrated about the marshlands at the head of Fundy in the area of the present day New Brunswick/Nova Scotia border. By the 1750s, thousands of acres had been reclaimed and Minas Basin alone supported a population of forty-five hundred.

There are two opposing views of the Acadians of that era. According to which account one listens to, they were a hardworking, religious people who were only interested in raising their families and working their land — both activities that they excelled at.

The other view is that they were an illiterate community of malcontents kept in a permanent state of near rebellion against the English Crown, abetted by their priests and with the cooperation of the local Mi'kmaq.

Somewhere in between doubtless lies the truth. Like common folk everywhere, they were caught up in history's upheavals, and probably just wanted to be left alone.

Unfortunately for them, the English, whose hold on Acadia was more nominal than factual, were subject to continuous raids by French led native attacks. Although these attacks were instigated by Quebec City and led by French Canadian officers they relied heavily on warrior/missionaries like Father Germain at St. Anne's (Fredericton) and Father Le Loutre of Chignecto for enlisting the natives. These priests were practically full time political activists who received their orders not from their bishops but from their governors. The fact that they were also leaders in the Acadian communities where they lived must make one skeptical of the settlers supposed lack of involvement.

We have a clear picture of Acadian life in this period. It was a life of unrelenting hard work, but with a strong sense of community that allowed them to enjoy the fruits of their labour. Summer saw them working on their farms and their dykes. When winter made work in the woods possible, they would cut their wood for fuel and fencing and so on.

Fish and game were plentiful; the rivers and the Bay teemed with salmon, bass, shad and eels.

On high ground, they planted orchards of apples, plums and cherries. While the men worked the farms growing their food, the womenfolk worked hard raising the children, spinning and weaving the cloth for their clothing.

Villages were like an extended family. Newlyweds for instance would have a house built for them and some livestock donated to get them started. Formal schooling seems to have been limited and the literacy rate was probably low, but certainly they had achieved a quality of life remarkable for that day.

Staying neutral is never easy and when the English took over power in Acadia, the Acadians were hopelessly caught between two fires. The English, uneasy at finding a large group of potential rebels in their midst, claimed them as subjects and tried repeatedly to make them take an oath of allegiance. At the same time, the French, from their strongholds in Quebec and Louisbourg in Cape Breton, continued to urge them to be faithful to the French cause and religion. Every time the question would arise, lengthy discussions would take place between the English authorities and the Acadians who were normally represented by their clergy. The roadblock to any agreement was always the same. Few of them were prepared to take an oath that could perhaps force them to take up arms against their own kind.

Talks would eventually break down, the priests would return to their parishes still uncommitted, likewise the English would return to Port Royal and later to Halifax, Acadia's capital, frustrated in their attempts to neutralize the Acadians once more. Any chance of the two sides coming to an agreement was in no way helped by the strong pressure that the English felt from severely Protestant New England centered in Boston.

At one point, becoming increasingly unnerved at the continuous pressure, the Acadians considered pulling up stakes and moving to Cape Breton. There they would be under the protection of the French who held the fortress at Louisbourg. Louisbourg was by far the most important fortress on the east coast, governing, as it did, all access to the interior through the St. Lawrence River, but this fact did not deter London, with a dazzling piece of diplomacy, from trading it back to the French for Madras! When the Acadians saw the available land however, they elected to take their chances where they were, rather than starve in Cape Breton. A fateful decision? Perhaps, perhaps not. Louisbourg was taken back by a force under Wolfe three years later in 1758. Anyway, another factor in their consideration may have been that they had moved to their present location in the first place to escape the constant turmoil around Port Royal; fortresses attracted activity and they just wanted to be left in peace.

When it finally happened, events unfolded with devastating swiftness. The happenings at Grand Pré in Nova Scotia present the most vivid description of the destruction of a thriving community. The techniques may have varied slightly from place to place, but the end results were the same.

In the fall of 1755, a Colonel Winslow, described by some as a half-educated, bigoted army commander, arrived in Grand Pré on the shores of Minas Basin along with an armed force. The troops took up position on a slight rise around the village church and watched as the villagers uneasily went about their daily chores, doubtless wondering what was going to follow.

Even the hardened Winslow started to have misgivings about the monstrosity he was going to commit. The sight of the villagers reaping their harvests and the children playing in the orchards must have given him second thoughts. "A fine day," he writes, "The inhabitants busy about their harvest."[1] However his instructions from Governor Lawrence in Halifax were clear.

The following day, Winslow called all the men and boys from the surrounding area to meet at the church to hear the final decision of the King. Expecting, no doubt, that they would be urged once again to take the oath of allegiance they complied without much argument. There would be the usual negotiations, delegations back and forth — the priests would tell them what to do and take care of matters.

The Expulsion of the Acadians

The colonel's proclamation droned on: "...lands and tenements. Cattle of all kinds and livestock..." It suddenly sunk in and a murmur ran round the church as those who understood translated for those who did not. They were being dispossessed of everything they owned — even their country. They were virtually stateless!

Winslow, to avoid any chance of rebellion, had the men marched in five groups of fifty to five waiting ships. The separation of men from their families and from their lovers had started. In one form or another this scene was repeated all over Acadia. All in all, some fourteen thousand Acadians were uprooted and distributed among the colonies to the south.

Many tried to escape into the woods or move on to more remote areas where they might evade the soldiers of the Crown. Pursuit was relentless and most were forced out of hiding by exposure and hunger. The troops' instructions were to use any means of compulsion and to deprive any who might escape of shelter and support, by burning houses and destroying any means of sustenance — some of the richest land in North America lay in smoking ruins.

It was not long, however, before the tenacity of these people made itself known. Almost immediately, from wherever they had been transported, they started drifting back. Indeed at least half of them tried to return. Some stayed in Louisiana and came to be known as 'Cajuns'. One group never made it out of the Bay of Fundy. Under the leadership of Charles Belliveau the prisoners overpowered the crew of the ship transporting them to South Carolina and sailed back into the St. John River. They were able to make contact with the forces of De Boishebert, who moved them back and out of harm's way, deep into the interior.

43

The Expulsion, as it came to be known, was carried out in the most cynical and inhumane manner. No effort was made to keep families together; in fact there were very likely deliberate moves to keep the prisoners off balance by separating them from their families.

There is no shortage of tales of hardship and brutality that arose out of the Expulsion; needless killings, broken relationships, humanity's behaviour at its worst.

For two months, three shiploads of deportees were forbidden to land in Philadelphia. When they were finally allowed to go ashore, there were 217 left living of the original 450.

In the late 1600s, Joseph de Villebon, Governor of Acadia, had built a fort where the Nashwaak River runs into the St. John, a vital link in the trade route to the Miramichi. They were joined by more Acadians around 1730 and escapees from the Expulsion in 1755. They had been fortunate enough to escape the attention of Monckton's dragnet in the Fall of 1758 when he had been turned back at Grimross (Gagetown) for fear of getting caught in the ice. Their good fortune was short-lived.

In January the following year, they became the focus of a Captain McCardy. Setting out from Fort Frederick (W. Saint John), the Captain and his men started upriver on the ice. When McCardy was accidentally killed by a falling tree, command of the unit shifted to his second-in-command, Lt. Moses Hazen.

When they arrived at St. Anne's at the mouth of the Nashwaak, they found the settlement deserted. Undeterred, Hazen destroyed 147 houses and all their outbuildings, leaving the inhabitants without food or shelter in the midst of winter. Many survived the incredible hardships but some less fortunate fell into Lt. Hazen's hands. He killed and scalped six of the settlers and took prisoner four men, two women and three children. History records the scalped victims to be Nastasie Paré, daughter of community leader Joseph Bellefontaine, her three children and the wife and child of Michel Bellefontaine.

General Amherst promoted Hazen to captain for a job well done, but had the good grace to express regrets when he heard the full story. Some of the escapees moved yet further up the river. Apart from a small trading post, the area was left clear to await the next wave of settlers, who would not arrive on the scene for another twenty-five years.

With help from the Malecites, those Acadians who had escaped the massive round-up, but thrust out of their traditional homeland, found new homes in the upper reaches of the St. John around the Madawaska. They pushed up the north shore and occupied lands that were out of the reach of the English navy.

From the early 1600s there had been Acadian settlements at the sites of present day Buctouche, Richibucto, and Bathurst, but there is no reference to any settlement on the Restigouche by Acadians or any mention at all until the Battle of Restigouche in 1760.

By this time, the French were rapidly losing their grip on their North American colonies. Nobody fought this rearguard action more stoutly than Charles de Boishebert.

Even before the Expulsion, Boishebert had been a pebble in the English boot, carrying out continuous attacks on isolated settlements. With the French fort at Beauséjour (near Sackville) fallen in 1755, the marshlands were secure, so a Captain Rous was sent to Saint John with three twenty-gun ships to flush out Boishebert. Boishebert withdrew upriver building a fort at the Nerepis and from this base helped a great many Acadians escape the Expulsion by moving them into less accessible areas, until he was himself driven from the river by Monckton.

For sheer misfortune the Commandant Boishebert was notable even by Acadian standards. Awakening from a sound sleep in his hospital room at Quebec city, he was the first to look out of the window and see the English army lined up on the plains of Abraham. The date was September 13th, 1759. Months later, still refusing to surrender, he was forced to watch as the final nail was driven into the French coffin at the mouth of the Restigouche River. Captain John Byron, grandfather of poet Lord Byron, commanding a squadron of English ships out of Louisbourg, cut off a French fleet of stores ships and their escorts from entering the St. Lawrence. He forced them into Baie Chaleur, and captured two French vessels pushing the remainder into the estuary of the Restigouche. Byron followed them into the river where he destroyed the shore batteries and either sank or captured the remainder of the fleet.

With his hard-fought cause hopelessly lost, the doughty warrior Boishebert took himself back to France where he was promptly thrown into the Bastille for suspected complicity in Superintendant of New France, François Bigot's, systematic fleecing of the public purse in Quebec. Boishebert was eventually cleared but not before serving fifteen months time in the cells.

His was the last attempt to hold the province of Acadia for France. There must have been times when he wondered if it was worth all the trouble. The whole French venture into North America was carried out at huge expense and correspondingly little return. In the critical early days under the guidance of Cardinal Richelieu, France was more interested in capitalizing on the Hapsburg's preoccupation with the Thirty Years' War that engulfed Germany from 1618 to 1648. Perhaps, because they chose to try to continue structuring North American society in the image of France, there had been no steady growth of emigrants from the Mother Country. The feudal system was alive and well in France — they did not need to come to Canada to find it. As the French colonies were losing their strength, the colonies of New England were becoming more and more vigorous. The New Englanders were much more committed to colonizing and much more cohesive in their efforts. The numbers tell the story. By 1685, there were approximately one hundred and fifty thousand English, as opposed to twelve thousand French and the gap kept widening.

There have been claims that in ordering the expulsion Governor Lawrence was acting without the official sanction of the government in London. Very possibly the orders came from Boston since most of the soldiery were New Englanders. Fingers have been pointed back and forth; some have actually tried to justify the whole action — "necessity knows no law." No restitution was ever given for the lands lost. Only at Memramcook and Fox Creek were the Acadians allowed to return to their old communities. No disciplinary action was taken against English officers who exceeded their authority. Governor Lawrence himself received five thousand acres (2,000 ha) of Acadian land for his trouble.

By 1763 the British held sway in North America and the Duke of Marlborough's successes over Louis XIV in the first decade of the century had brought a temporary peace between the fractious neighbours. It would not last long — it never did, but many Acadians took advantage of the situation and started drifting back. They found their lands overtaken by the English and scattered throughout the area wherever they could find land. For most it would be in the coastal regions of the east and northeast.

The return of the Acadians after their expulsion bore with it a curious postscript. Leprosy suddenly appeared on the Acadian peninsula – a remote piece of coastline projecting northeast into the Gulf of St. Lawrence from the mouth of the Miramichi. It is not certain where this disease came from – it is normally associated with tropical or at least temperate climates. That people returning from the southern United States may have brought it back with them, is as good a theory as any. There were a few cases among settlers of Scottish and Irish backgrounds but the victims were overwhelmingly Acadian.

The first documented death from leprosy occurred in 1828 and it was not long before authorities felt it necessary to place eighteen more cases in quarantine. Sheldrake Island in the Miramichi east of Chatham, which had been used as a quarantine station for immigrants, presented itself as a convenient spot to hide them. This installation was placed under the care of a board consisting of a doctor, three businessmen and a priest (the only Acadian among them). Once on Sheldrake Island the lepers were left completely to their own devices: no care, no medical attention, absolutely no effort to make their miserable lives more bearable. Not surprisingly the inmates took every opportunity to escape and when winter came and the river froze, any remaining took off across the ice. One by one they were hunted down and returned to the island, and guards were posted to patrol the island's shores. The 'patients' thereupon burned the building down. The board, just as obstinate rebuilt. (Among the three businessmen on the board were Andrew Rankine and Joseph Cunard. Remember the names.)

In 1848 the facility was moved to Tracadie, and medical assistance was finally provided – of a sort. Dr. Billois moved in and promptly announced that his charges were not lepers at all, but simply suffering from syphilis. He even made some apparent cures, giving his patients excellent care – dressings changed twice daily, and enforcing rigorous hygiene. Unfortunately all or most of his cures came out of remission, and the Province refused to pay him his dues. Paying physicians by results may be an interesting concept for making cutbacks to the health care system, but the good doctor's removal did nothing for the leper's plight. Even the wrong treatment is sometimes better than no treatment at all.

It was not until the 1860's that they were given a resident doctor and the second of these, Dr. Alfred Corbett Smith stayed for thirty-four years. Then their luck really took a turn for the better when a group of nuns from Quebec - Les Hospitalieres de Saint Joseph came to Tracadie, and the disease was eventually brought under control. The last two cases from the Acadian Peninsula died there in 1934, but by the turn of the century the federal government had assumed responsibility, and from that time, until the facility was closed down in 1965 the only patients lodged there were occasional immigrants inflicted with the disease.

In a miracle of ethnic survival, the Acadians have thrived in New Brunswick since those dark days. Today they account for forty percent of the population and they are still adamant that they are not French Canadian, but Acadian.

Five

The English

Now, with the decline of French military power and the Acadians for the most part removed from the scene, the country was left wide open for whoever wanted it and settlers started drifting in from the colonies to the south. With the continuous threat of French or Indian attack gone, one by one the old Acadian settlements were taken over by New Englanders, including the rich marshlands that had been developed so painstakingly.

Not all the newcomers were English. A group of Germans from Pennsylvania took over land on the Petitcodiac River near where Moncton stands today. Descendants of the Stieffs, Lutz's, Jonas's are still to be found as Steeves, Lutes and Jones. Some Scots led by William Davidson and John Cort founded a community on the Miramichi.

Trading posts sprang up on the Nepisquit and Restigouche Rivers. Permanent communities at St. Stephen and St. Andrews developed on Passamaquoddy Bay and the islands of Campobello and Deer Island attracted others. Most importantly, however, for the eventual development of New Brunswick, in the absence of roadways, the great St. John River system, remained the central avenue for communication and trade.

In 1762, James Simonds arrived at the mouth of the river from Passamaquoddy where he had been trading and fishing. Originally, from Newburyport, Massachusetts, he was every inch a trader. He set up some lime kilns and a thriving fishery, and in partnership with William Hazen and James White, he expanded his trade into the lumber business. The forests of New Brunswick, at that time, abounded with tall straight pines. We read descriptions of woods like parkland where a horse and cart could be driven among the great trees.

Others came to join Simonds, Francis Peabody, Johnathan Leavitt, Hugh Quinton and fifteen other men and women came to establish themselves. Some were able to stay in Fort Frederick on the West Side — opposite the remains of the old fort where Francoise La Tour made her stand — until their accommodations were built. This was the embryo of what would shortly become a thriving city, but for now it was still an outpost under almost daily threats by privateers. Whether they sailed under French, Dutch or English flags they made coastal life in these parts miserable for years and would continue to do so for years to come.

At the ending of hostilities between French and English there were many military officers who had been disbanded from Royal service and who wished to stay in New Brunswick. Bureaucracy is sometimes slow to learn and when grants were offered to these gentlemen the conditions bore a startling resemblance to the French Seigniory system — and proved to be about as effective.

A survey crew under Israel Perley was sent up river by Simonds' friends in Essex County, Massachusetts with the intention of laying out a townsite at the location of the burned out St. Anne's settlement. No sooner had they arrived there, however, when they were joined by a party of Malicetes in full war paint claiming first rights to the land. Convinced, Perley and his crew fell back down the river several miles and decided that they could be just as happy at that location.

Two townsites on the Saint John river became the focus of attention for development in the 1760s: Maugerville and Grimross (Gagetown). Maugerville had a good start, but never really developed despite its favoured location close to Fredericton. For two decades, Maugerville survived as the business centre of Sunbury County which for practical purposes meant New Brunswick, since in those days the Province of Nova Scotia had so designated almost the whole region. The constant threat of springtime flooding had the developers looking elsewhere. Half way between Saint John and St. Anne (Fredericton), opposite old Fort Jemseg at the entrance to Grand Lake, they found a near perfect spot and Grimross was groomed for greatness.

The site of Grimross may have been near perfect, but it was not perfect enough because it did not quite lie on the Saint John river. It was actually about half a mile (700 m.) up a navigable dead-end creek, separated from the main waterway by a narrow strip of intervale land. For some reason, this seemingly trivial obstacle was enough to deter people from using it. There was even an attempt to cut a gap through to the main channel but to no avail.

In 1764, a group of about sixty disbanded army officers met to form "the Saint John River Society." Its aim was to take advantage of the Crown's land settlement offer. The terms were very much like those offered under the old seigniory system. They were required to settle "four protestants for each 1000 acres…" A quarter of their grant having to be settled in each of the first four years. One can gather from this account that religious tolerance was not foremost in their thoughts. These were people of solid puritan stock from New England. The first Baptist would not arrive in Central New Brunswick until

View of Waterloo Row, Fredericton, during flood of 1887   *Courtesy: PANB #P5-283*

1799 and no Roman Catholic or even Church of Scotland ministers were licensed to officiate at marriages until 1822.

Governor Lawrence of 'The Expulsion' fame was only slightly ambiguous in his 1759 appeal to prospective settlers from New England when he listed among the advantages of life. "Full liberty of conscience, paptists excepted...; and all such dissenters shall be excused from any taxes levied for the support of the established church of England," meaning the Anglican Church.

Unfortunately, these schemes attracted more speculators than settlers. Few of the St. John River Society's shareholders had the slightest intention of settling there themselves. It would be much better to lease out the land to good hard-working tenants, who would clear the land, do the farming and pay the rent on time. As with the Seigniories the plan worked out better on paper than in real life. In time, the grants were all revoked for non-fulfilment. There had been some settlement, but in nothing like the numbers anticipated. Grimross, now Gagetown, became a part of the great landbank awaiting the next wave of immigrants. They would not be long coming.

When rebellion broke out in the lower colonies in 1776, the new inhabitants of the Saint John River valley had a lot to ponder. They had come directly from areas where the majority favoured the rebel cause and many had friends and relatives fighting against the British. A group met at Maugerville and decided to send resolutions to Boston supporting the new regime. Somehow the word passed to an unlikely brace of characters from Cumberland County, Nova Scotia — Johnathan Eddy and John Allen. These men, heavily committed to the Rebel cause raised some volunteers at Machias, Maine, and marched on Fort Beausejour. They were joined by about three hundred dissident settlers, including those from Maugerville who had signed the resolution, and a few natives. Armed with

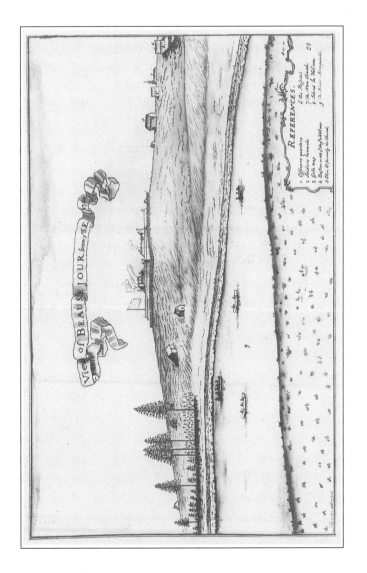

Fort Beauséjour (artist's drawing)   *Courtesy: PANB #P4/3/0029*

little more than blind faith, they laid siege to the fort. It was a classic 'dog chasing bus' situation. They tried to goad the garrison into coming out to fight, but the commandant Colonel Gorham could find little reason to do so. Help promised to the rebels never materialized; but help for the garrison did. A small contingent of regular force soldiers landed nearby under cover of darkness. Stealing up on the sleeping rebels, the troops easily overwhelmed them, and in half an hour the rebellion had passed into history. Many of the rebels took to the woods and straggled home as best they could; the rest were herded off to Halifax as prisoners.

That outcome might have been the end of it had they not set up a rebel trading post in competition with James Simonds. Simonds complained to Halifax; and the Governor, now seeing the seriousness of the situation, sent Major Studholme to flush them out. The rebels apart from three men all took the oath of allegiance. One of the holdouts, Rev. Seth Noble was instrumental in founding Bangor, Maine.

Six
⁙

The Loyalists

In the lower colonies, the relations between colonists and Britain had become more and more strained. Since earliest colonial times, there had been a touchiness in the New Englander's independence, and a general ignorance, tempered with arrogance towards them in London. Leadership was at a weak point under George III and the three men he chose to conduct England's most important war since 1066 did not help much. Lord North was so retiring by nature that he discouraged people from calling him Prime Minister; he also proudly proclaimed his total ignorance of anything military. Lord Germain did have a military background — he had been cashiered out of the army as unfit for service after the Battle of Minden for refusal to obey orders. Between these two was Lord Sandwich, the First Sea Lord, who was capable enough when he could be found — his favourite pursuits were chasing women and gambling. None of these men had the faintest idea of the type of person they were running up against, sharing complete contempt of the rebel forces, and ignoring the wealth of talent, ready to help, among the Loyalists.

The colonists had come to New England in the first place to escape religious oppression and created an extremely viable economic and political entity out of wilderness. They had watched the English king go to the executioner's block,

Cromwell's decade of dictatorship, the return of the monarchy, and Protestant kings replaced by Catholic kings and queens. Over the period of a century, much of the English colonist's engrained respect for the monarchy had dissipated.

The Revolutionary War, or War of Independence, was certainly both of those things, but it should be understood that it was also very much a civil war. The half million souls who now populated the colonies were overwhelmingly of British Isles stock and there were few families that had no ties to the other side of the Atlantic, where the war was extremely unpopular.

The war is a subject in itself and will not be dealt with beyond some discussion as to how the sides shaped up. Our concerns are twofold. Who were the Loyalists, and why were they Loyalists?

There is a common misconception that the Loyalists represented the elite of colonial life. This is a misconception that many descendants of the Loyalists have become quite comfortable with and have done little to dispel. About one hundred thousand colonials, roughly twenty percent of the population, took up the Loyalist cause for one reason or another.

They came from all walks of life. Loyalty to the Crown crossed social caste lines; even families were divided.

There is an element of truth in the charge of 'elitism'. Those who had held a special relationship with the mother country and had an interest, financial or otherwise, in continued English rule obviously took the Loyalist side. Included in this category would be Governors, judges, traders and their staffs who made their livelihood by dealing with firms in Britain. To say that this elite were wholeheartedly in favour of rule from London might not be true either. More likely, they wanted to be a part of a partnership that blended the best of both societies — the power and cultural traditions of a nation on the verge of world domination and the huge natural resources and vigor of a new country.

As in any civil war, local issues and simple 'peer pressure' played their part. In all probability most of the colonists would have been quite happy to be left alone, but got drawn into the fight anyway.

The Loyalist cause attracted a great many of the religious and cultural minorities in colonial life; this fact might seem surprising at first glance but they found much more freedom under the Crown than under the repressive and sternly Protestant society in British North America. These groups included immigrants from Germany, Holland, the British Isles themselves, Huguenots, Catholics and Quakers. Blacks were promised their freedom by the Crown and overwhelmingly supported the Loyalist cause.

If this curtailment of freedom may seem inconsistent with the slogan "life, liberty and the pursuit of happiness," it should be remembered that the Puritans had fought tenaciously for their own liberties, and those who achieve liberty are often remarkably stingy in offering it to others.

When the war was lost and the dust had settled, there were some forty to sixty thousand loyalists in the colonies that were totally dispossessed by the victorious rebels. There was deep resentment towards them because of their involvement with the Crown, and there was no forgiveness for them. They were hounded and persecuted unmercifully until it became plain that their complete removal was the only viable solution.

Under the Peace Treaty, the English, with a sensitivity that could not always be relied upon, did their best to take care of their ruined supporters. Their commissioners pressed the

Americans to make some provision for these refugees by restoring confiscated property and rights of citizenship. The Americans, however, had won the war. There was no need for them to make any concessions and they made none.

Far from it. The Loyalists were treated as the vilest of traitors. They were subjected to harassment and torture, even death, for fighting for what they believed in. This barbaric treatment shown to them certainly added to the flood of refugees heading to the enclave at New York where people were gathering for emigration to other parts of the Empire.

There is no question that rebel behaviour towards the defeated Loyalists was beyond excuse, but the king's men were capable of atrocities too. A notable example was the story of a Colonel David Fanning who openly boasted of the occasions that he had gunned down defenseless people who found themselves at his mercy. Fanning came to New Brunswick and in later years could be seen sharing refreshments with the great turncoat, General Benedict Arnold, at the exchange coffee house on King Street in Saint John. He was one of only three men excluded from the general pardon offered loyalists by the North Carolina legislature. His brother Edmund Fanning became the Governor of Prince Edward Island — at that time still known as The Island of St. John.

The Loyalists were faced with the alternatives of life under the "tyranny of an exulting enemy or settle a new country." Repatriation to Britain after a hundred years of colonial life was not an option for most. The uprooted families would have had huge problems adapting to the complicated social structures of British life and only about two thousand tried it, mostly new arrivals. London started to cast about for alternative spots among her colonies. The task was gigantic in its scope and complexity and needed superlative leadership. The task fell to Sir Guy Carleton.

Considering the problems he was facing, Sir Guy did a truly remarkable job. Three agents were dispatched to Nova Scotia to search for suitable land. They surveyed the land around Port Royal (now Annapolis) and crossed over Fundy to the St. John River. They travelled upstream as far as Maugerville and discovered that there was land waiting for settlement everywhere.

Meanwhile, the Loyalists had started to congregate in New York in unexpectedly large numbers as prisoners of war were released and others came out of hiding. They needed supplies. They needed destinations and shipping for themselves and their belongings. Carleton had to achieve all of these things in the midst of an extremely hostile environment and an outbreak of small pox. If everything did not go entirely according to plan it should not be surprising. The fact that the evacuation was carried out at all speaks very highly of this capable man.

In 1783, ten thousand Loyalists and their descendants arrived in Saint John aboard two fleets. With them came thirty-four hundred soldiers of the British American regiments and five hundred disbanded men. They came from all walks of life and brought with them many talents. They were mostly of British Isles stock, but among them were a good supply of Germans, Dutch and Huguenots. There were also among them two hundred and twenty blacks and not all freed. Although the Crown had promised freedom for blacks, there was small print stipulating that the offer only applied to slaves owned by the rebels.

There was still little or no political structure to help in the settling of this massive influx of humanity. New Brunswick was still known as Sunbury County, a section of Nova Scotia, entitled to elect two members to the assembly in Halifax. No help was forthcoming, Halifax was busy enough with its own rush of refugees. Governor Parr did, however, find time to name the community to the east of the harbour, Parrtown; the west side of the harbour became known as Carleton in recognition of Sir Guy's efforts on their behalf.

The first fleet arrived in Saint John on May 10th, 1783, and the East side of the Harbour became a tent city overnight. The air rang with the sound of axes as the settlers cleared their lots for more permanent accommodation. A survey map was produced which overlaid a grid on the outline of Saint John (Parrtown) between the river and Courtenay Bay in the east. Whoever created this masterpiece of town planning had clearly never laid eyes on the ground involved. Looking at Saint John, even today after two hundred years of cutting and blasting, it is easy to imagine what the terrain must have looked like then. Nevertheless, progress was made under the watchful eye of Major Gilfred Studholme, commander of the garrison at Fort Howe. He looked after the distribution of lumber and tools to the new arrivals. Major Studholme was eventually given a large grant on the Kennebecasis. It was well deserved; no one at that time worked harder for the security and success of the future city.

On the other hand Governor Parr, whose name briefly graced the new community, went out of his way to disrupt any attempt at development of any place other than Halifax; and helped himself liberally to lands for the use of himself and his cronies.

The luckiest, or perhaps the canniest, of the first invasion would have to be among the passengers of the *Union* who gave the gathering crowd round Upper Cove one quick look and headed upriver. They came to roost at Kingston Creek, a beautiful spot just a few miles from all the hubbub. They met friendly natives who made them welcome and kept them supplied with moosemeat. By the end of Fall, they all had built their cabins and spent an immeasurably more comfortable winter than their companions who had elected to remain in Saint John. The Kingston Loyalists built Trinity Church which survives today as the oldest standing church in New Brunswick.

The majority, however, who had stayed to take their chances in Saint John, had things a little harder. Lots were doled out by lottery. This plan sounds fine in theory, but in practice created endless complications. The way the city plan had been laid out, a family could find the lot it had picked clinging to the side of a cliff, buried in a swamp, or in some other way unsuitable for development. Others contributed to the confusion by astutely entering a second lottery before the results of the first were announced. This may have been a good way to 'hedge one's bets', but did nothing to help in the orderly transfer of land. Others, too impatient to let matters take their own course, took things into their own hands, heading upriver and making themselves at home on the first unoccupied land they could find. Yet others saw fit to sell their lots of land and squat wherever they could. Then there were those who sold their lots and invested the proceeds in other diversions.

There were about thirty-five hundred black Loyalists to accommodate; England's promise of freedom for blacks who fought for the cause had brought them flocking to the flag! Only two hundred of these came to New Brunswick on assurances from Guy Carleton that they would be given land on equality with the whites. He meant well but the reality was bitter disappointment.

If the less influential whites had trouble getting adequate land, the blacks had it even worse. The majority got no land at all, and those who did found themselves sitting it out until the whites got their grants. They usually had to make do with a piece of land that was very small, very bad or both. Some land was simply too far out in the bush to be of any use to anyone.

In any event, many of the blacks had no experience with farm work and were ill-suited for it. Others lucky enough to obtain a tiny lot in Saint John found that no one, black or white, could work at a trade in the city without being granted 'Freeman Status' — a selective licensing practice that survived well into the twentieth century — an avenue that was invariably closed to them. Having little or no recourse to the courts, they were habitually shorted on their provisions and often had to work on the roads to survive. Cheated at every turn, some were forced to sign their freedom away. Despite a hungry labour market that was paying high wages to whites, many blacks were forced to lives in semi-slavery as indentured workers.

Old attitudes about slavery died hard among the Loyalists; many indeed still owned slaves. So this so-called enlightened society carried with it many of the restraints and prejudices the blacks had hoped were left behind.

Frustrated, Thomas Peters, the black leader who had brought the two hundred blacks over from Annapolis on Carleton's assurances, organized an exodus of blacks from both New Brunswick and Nova Scotia to Sierra Leone in 1791. The exodus of almost twelve hundred of Peters' followers — about a third of the total black population - came as a shock to the white population, who realized belatedly that they were losing a sizeable pool of cheap labour. It also came as something of a shock to the British government, which was footing the bill for transporting the evacuees to West Africa. Despite all attempts to dissuade them from taking this step, and all the dire predictions of the authorities, they were unshakable in their determination. An end to the injustices and frustrations of life in New Brunswick and Nova Scotia and a guarantee of no return to slavery, were evidently worth any hardship that might have to be endured in Sierra Leone.

For those who stayed, it would be a long hard battle. By organizing their own church groups and schooling, they were able for the first time to form a cohesive community, enabling them bit by bit to pursue their rights. Perhaps because schooling came under British army direction during the early years, integration came early to Fredericton. In 1797, a school was opened by Major Brannen for forty-one pupils, thirty white and eleven black.

On June 29th, the second fleet arrived from New York causing further congestion in the new settlement. As more and more people arrived, lots became divided and sub-divided, making cultivation impossible and causing endless confusion and frustration. Saint John, or Parrtown, was bursting at the seams.

If ever there was a good reason for Loyalists *not* to be elitist it would have been the first two years in the city. They obviously had no means of supporting themselves and provision had to be made by Sir Guy Carleton for their survival with the mother country. Gratitude, in Britain, was gradually shifting to indifference and irritation. They had virtually forced their colonies into rebellion, lost the resulting war and were feeling disaffected by their whole North American experience. Between the growing indifference of the English and the hatred of the Americans, Carleton was a miracle worker.

Wherever possible, the Loyalists sailed from New York issued with a year's ration consisting of one pound of bread, twelve ounces of pork or twenty-one ounces of beef per day for each man and woman. Half that amount was each child's ration over and above these provisions, which seem generous enough. They were issued with tents, blankets, clothing and necessary tools such as axes and spades and upon arrival supplies for husbandry and building were provided. At that time boards and shingles had to be imported for home building, but the wood for framing had to be cut from the lots themselves. For years after, the sidewalks were cluttered with stumps.

There were probably about nine thousand people who spent that first winter clustered round the harbour in Saint John. By the onset of winter, fifteen hundred houses had been built while the remainder of the settlers roughed it out in tents and huts. Life must have been nightmarish trying to keep one's family warm and fed with nothing but 'green' wood for fuel. In a community of closely packed wood frame houses, many of which had wooden outbuildings and stables full of hay and straw, a fire of major proportions was just a matter of time. It happened sooner than any would have wished, a scant year after the first landing. For a long time the most unpopular man in town must have been the settler at the corner of Princess and Wentworth, who, while burning brush, let it get away on him. Picked up by a brisk wind, the blaze quickly spread to Courtenay Bay, west to Charlotte Street and north across King Square. It raced across the valley and went clear over to the Kennebecasis River. Many of the cabins and huts built by the settlers were reduced to ashes and much of the timber needed for construction and heat was lost. Fortunately the population was resilient and rich in talent, and this fire caused only a minor setback in the town's development.

Plans were made for the partition of the province of Nova Scotia to reflect the realities of the day. Poor communications and conflicting interests demanded that the Province be split in two, and a boundary was established at the Missaquash River. New Ireland was one name proposed for the new province, but it lacked appeal to George III, so it was named after one of his German Duchys whose troops had fought so well for him in the Revolutionary War.

On August 16th, 1784, the Province of New Brunswick was proclaimed with Sir Guy Carleton's brother, Thomas, its first Governor. He was an excellent choice showing the same dedication to the welfare of the people that his brother always had. However, his first action astounded the new residents of Parrtown when he proclaimed St. Anne's, ninety miles up the river, as the new capital. It was renamed Frederick's Town after H.R.H. Frederic, Duke of York.

His reasoning for the move was that Fredericton, being at the head of navigation for large vessels would make an ideal springboard for the development of the interior. Its distance from the sea also made it more secure from attack. The grants for disbanded army units had been concentrated in that area in case the Americans should attack overland. General Benedict Arnold of the Loyal American Legion had grants on Waterloo Row and Kingsclear. His aide-de-camp Captain Nathan Frink had one nearby.

Settlement of this area by the two thousand troops had not been smooth. Winter started on November 2nd, 1783, with a six-inch snowfall and found many without shelter. We read of mothers keeping their children alive by heating rocks and boards to give them warmth. Many were forced to brave the winter in tents using pine boughs and snow for insulation against the bitter cold.

Other areas had other problems. Loyalists settling in St. Stephen and St. Andrews had American agents moving among them, telling them not to get too comfortable, that the border was going to be moved to the Magaguadavic River twenty-five miles (40 km.) to the east.

Guardian of the people or not, Thomas Carleton had a way of getting things done the way he wanted. The Colonial Secretary in London, Lord Sydney, wanted Carleton to call a general assembly as soon as possible. His waiting room at the ministry was crowded with some of the wealthier Loyalists seeking compensation for their claims, and he therefore felt some urgency in setting up some means of handling the problem locally. Carleton, on the other hand, wishing to avoid the restraints of democracy until he was good and ready, had stalled on calling the assembly and busied himself organizing all the counties and parishes, installing his own appointments. His mistrust of the trading class was deeply embedded in him and they were a powerful entity in Saint John. He felt, probably correctly, that the traders were more interested in laying their hands on as much of the public money that was floating about as they could, than they were in the long range development of the province. They were more attuned to offshore trading than development of the interior.

The incorporation of Saint John as the first chartered city of British North America did little to mollify the citizens, especially when they found that their new city charter allowed for appointment of the Mayor by the Governor. An opposition party sprang up under the leadership of Elias Hardy, a New York lawyer who already had earned a reputation for bucking the establishment.

The first exercise of democracy in Saint John was not promising. It also underlined the strong divisions in Loyalist society.

The east side of the harbour became factionalized between the 'Upper Cove' elite and the 'Lower Cove' tradesmen and working classes. The Upper Covers, centred around present day Market Slip, suspected that revolutionaries lurked among the Lower Covers. The Lower Covers suspected that the Upper Covers had plans to return to the old class system. There is little doubt that the elite *did* feel that effective government

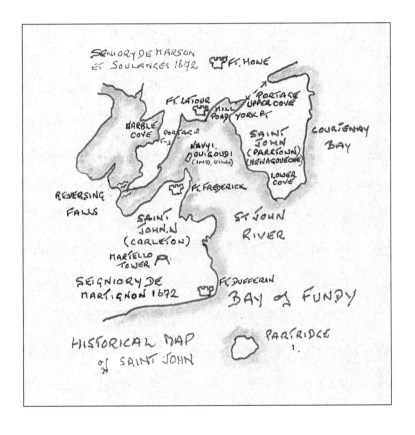

HISTORICAL MAP
of SAINT JOHN

could be carried on without a lot of irritating debate and they
set out to prove it.

When it became apparent that the vote was going the wrong
way the Upper Covers stayed calm and saw to it that all the
polling stations were placed squarely in their own territory.
There was a riot and the troops had to be called down from
Fort Howe to settle the Lower Covers down. The polls were
closed for several days.

When voting resumed and the polls were closed, the Governor was disappointed to find that the Lower Covers had still
won the election by a one hundred vote margin. Undismayed,
the voters list was carefully scrutinized and two hundred votes
were eliminated, ensuring victory for the the Governor's team.

It might be supposed that these measures would have resulted in more rioting, or at least some lively political action,
but it seems that the Lower Covers had been satisfied to make
their point. There would be no return to the old class system
in New Brunswick.

It is hard to overestimate the impact made by some fourteen thousand immigrants into a society that to this point had
only numbered about three thousand people, who had been
divided more or less equally between English and Acadian background, with a few hundred natives. It was still not a big population, but one that had significance far outreaching its numbers.

First, the Loyalist migration ensured the existence of two
nations in North America. In the second place, it probably
also guaranteed the survival of the French Canadians as a cultural group. If the Americans had been able to conquer Canada,
the French would almost certainly have been swamped by mil-
lions of English speakers who had no interest in preserving
their culture.

Johann Lorenz Rugendas?, German
Benedict Arnold, after 1776
mezzotint on laid paper 35.7 x 12.1 cm (plate)
Courtesy: NBM, Webster Canadiana Collection, W85

The unfortunate man who had set fire to the fledgling City of Saint John in 1784 may not have been a favourite among his neighbours, but the book on unpopularity was re-written by the infamous Benedict Arnold; and not only in the United States.

Arnold lived in New Brunswick for about six years as the Province's most notable, if not well-loved refugee. If anything, he found himself to be only marginally more popular there than he had made himself among the Americans. To this day American hackles rise at the very mention of his name. This ever complex, sometimes inspired man deserves a note.

Arnold was born in Norwich, Connecticut, in 1741 and ran away from home at the age of fourteen to serve in the Seven Years' War. He joined the rebellion 1776, fighting with courage and flair at the Battle of Ticonderoga, sharing command with Ethan Allen. In the same year he was also wounded in the daring but unsuccessful raid on Quebec City on New Year's Eve.

Somehow, despite Arnold's unquestioned valour and capability, everyone was singing the praises of Allen, and to his further disgust he was bypassed for promotion. Arnold was not long to show his displeasure at this turn of events, and took his complaints to George Washington, who recognizing his talents, pitted him against the British General 'Johnny' Burgoyne at Saratoga.

Again much of the credit for this important victory went to someone else, this time General Horatio Gates. The more praise Gates received the deeper Arnold's resentment grew.

When the British withdrew from Philadelphia in 1778 Arnold was appointed Governor. However, even there his difficult personality got him into trouble, and he was soon facing a long list of misconduct charges. Eventually all but two of the charges were thrown out and even those two drew only a reprimand. Nevertheless he was stung by the experience. All this controversy notwithstanding Arnold was still considered to be one of the 'stars' of the Revolution, and Washington gave him command of the all important post at West Point on the Hudson River.

In all probability, the last straw in Arnold's dissillusionment with the rebels' cause was their alliance with France. He saw the pact with the hereditary foe of the Anglo-Saxons as nothing less than a plot to promote Roman Catholicism in the colonies. At the same time he felt that he had made significant strides in achieving some reconciliation through his own efforts.

In September 1780, Benedict Arnold crossed the lines into history as America's most hated turncoat. His price was the rank of Brigadier General in the British army, and the sum of £20,000 to compensate him for his lost properties. He then raised an armed force, the Loyal American Legion, leading them in numerous raids in Virginia and Connecticut.

In late 1781, Arnold escaped to England, where he stayed for four years before coming to Saint John, determined to establish himself in business. While in Saint John it seems that he was fairly well regarded among his peers, but heartily loathed by anyone over whom he held superiority — which was of course nearly everyone.

Arnold seems to have been well fixed financially — £20,000 was a good start in those days — and he built himself a store and warehouse in Lower Cove. He bought a number of properties around Saint John, and may have considered moving to Fredericton for a while, taking three lots on present day Waterloo Row, as well as his grant at nearby Kingsclear. One of his properties in Saint John, at the corner of King and Canter-

bury Streets, became the home of the Exchange Coffee House —
for years a popular meeting place in the city.

For the most part the problems that arose in his new home
seemed to stem from his business dealings. One cannot escape
the feeling that it would be more profitable to be Arnold's
lawyer than his business partner. Nehemiah Beckwith certainly
thought so.

Beckwith sold Arnold a ship, which was under construction, and the General promptly ordered extensive alterations
by a "gentleman's agreement'. The shipbuilder was not long
finding out who the gentleman was. Arnold refused to pay the
amount due, reasoning that Beckwith had gone well past the
agreed completion date, and made no allowances for the extra
work. Beckwith survived bankruptcy, but only just. Word
spreads fast in a small town and this incident surely made him
enemies in the young community.

Bits and pieces come to us from the newspapers of that
time — an advertisement by Arnold in *The Gazette* offers ..."a
£10 reward for the return of thirteen firkins of butter stolen
from the wrecked brigantine Lord Middleton."

It was an era of intense activity in the new city. Trade was
brisk with New England and the West Indies, but Arnold was
still having his problems. His store and warehouse in Lower
Cove — recently insured — burned to the ground resulting in
a loss of £1,000 on the building and £5,000 on the stock.

It is indicative of Arnold's popularity level that, when an
erstwhile partner named Hoyt accused the General of arson,
he was believed by one and all — especially his insurers. He
was forced to sue for slander and won his case, but the award
of £1 in damages seems to tell us where the judge's sympathies
lay. As a whole the people of Saint John were in full agreement

with the judge, and registered their dislike by burning the General in effigy outside his house. The Riot Act was read and the crowd was eventually dispersed by the militia.

Actually it is probable that Arnold did not in fact commit the crime of arson. There was no compelling evidence that he did, and some that he did not. In any event the trial finished him for Saint John. He sold his furniture at auction and returned to England with his longsuffering wife Peggy. Peggy was one of the few bright spots in his life. She *was* universally liked wherever his destiny took him, and if there was anything constant about him it is said to have been his love for her. Such may have been the case, but it did not stop him from leaving behind a mistress and two illegitimate children, at his death in 1801.

Life was not much kinder to the Arnolds in London, than it had been in the colonies. As always he attracted controversy, and came to be looked upon as something of an oddity, and generally avoided.

When the crowd burned him in effigy after the Hoyt case, he must have seen the sign fastened to the dummy. It read "TRAITOR !"

Nobody loves a turncoat.

Seven

❖

Shipbuilding

As the immigrants settled down in their new homeland, and order of sorts was established, the brand new Province set about changing itself from a backwoods society to an industrial entity. The first steps could have been more reassuring.

A lively business had opened up with Saint John acting as a go-between for American trade with the British West Indies, thus avoiding a British embargo placed on United States goods. Then in a scaling down of hostilities with the Americans, the British lifted their embargo on the new republic. Business in the city collapsed.

In another move that put the brakes on expansion, the Secretary of State in London, decided to stop the giving out of any more land grants. Immigration slowed to a trickle. Nevertheless Saint John was on the threshold of power and prosperity that would make it a world leader for the better part of the next century.

Shipbuilding in New Brunswick did not start under the Loyalists; it had been an important part of the pre-loyalist economy since the early 1770s. However among the new immigrants were a great number of people skilled in seafaring and shipbuilding trades. Shipyards sprang up all over the region.

Photographer Unknown: Canadian School **Revolving Light**, 1875 albumen print mounted on card 15.7 x 19.3 cm Gift of P.W.M. Brewster, 1932 (19151) *Courtesy: Collection of the NBM*

Shipbuilding had started with shipping lumber and masts to the British Isles. Napoleon had thrown a blockade across the entrance to the Baltic Sea, which was the main source of Britain's supply. Britain's groves of oaks had all but disappeared and, in any event, building their ships out of oak was incredibly expensive, resulting in vessels too small to be used economically for bulk cargoes. Since lumber was both plentiful and cheap all over eastern Canada, a great number of large ships started to be built in New Brunswick and Nova Scotia. Both ships and cargo would often be sold in Britain as a package; otherwise the ship would return with ballast or immigrants ready for another load.

In later years ships would be built for the cotton trade or for the whaling industry, but for years the cargo of choice would be pine masts and spars. In those days the New Brunswick pines stood tall and straight for well over a hundred feet. Representatives of the Royal Navy would scour the woods, marking every pine that they could find over two feet in diameter as property of the King's Armed Forces. This measure got all the attention it deserved; nevertheless, it lasted until 1811. Meanwhile landowners who were at all vulnerable made good and sure that none of their trees got to be that big.

From 1785, William Olive and his family built ships on the West Side of Saint John, and did so at a remarkable pace. Between 1822 and 1865, the Olive yard turned out no fewer than one hundred and twenty-five ships — a major operation. No doubt the family were glad that most of their launchings were less eventful than that of the *Belvedere* in 1835. According to a news item covering the happening, the ship, fully rigged, and decks awash with local celebrities, slipped smartly down the ways, into the water and — capsized, "adding extensively to the floating population of the harbour." The full skirts and cloaks of the guests kept them afloat until they could be rescued. Miraculously nobody seems to have drowned.

The Olive family were related by marriage to another shipbuilding family: the Stackhouses. The Stackhouse and MacLaughlin yard became well known for their *Dusty Miller* that for many years, made three round trips annually to the United Kingdom. This yard also had a reputation for building ships at high speed. In one remarkable effort one of their ships sailed for Britain, with a cargo of boards just eight weeks to the day from the time its keel was laid.

In 1839 the registered tonnage of new shipping out of Saint John was 28,538 tons. Twenty years later the figure had topped off at close to 60,000 tons — an amazing output for those days. Straight Shore — now known as Chesley Drive — was shipyards from one end to the other, but the sound of axes and adzes could also be heard far up the St. John and Kennebecasis rivers, all along the shore from St. Andrews to St. Martins; and up the eastern and north shores.

1851 saw the demand for shipping take another leap. Gold was found in Australia.

One year prior to that, James Smith laid the keel of a 1,625 ton ship, at his yard on the banks of Marsh Creek. Built of pine, oak, and hackmatack, she was intended for the timber trade. He named her the *Marco Polo*.

A superstitious owner might have consulted a fortune teller after a gale destroyed her framework, just as she was ready for planking. His worst fears would have been realized when the *Marco Polo* was launched on a spring tide in April 1851. Somehow she got away from her handlers, shot across the creek and fetched up in the mud on the far side. Here she stayed for two weeks, stubbornly resisting all attempts to move her. At the end of May, all straightened out — apart from a slight 'hog' in her hull, that she had picked up during her little adventure — she sailed for Liverpool. Her arrival was just in time to take part in the great Australian Gold Rush. Bought by the Black Ball line — who were probably ignorant of her short but interesting past — she was quickly refitted to carry a thousand passengers.

James Nichol 'Bully' Forbes, Marco Polo's new master, openly bragged around the Liverpool docks that he could sail her out to Australia and back in six months. A six-month trip was unheard of at that time, and his boast was treated with polite skepticism — no one laughed to his face. Anyone who dug into his pockets for money to lay against Forbes was going to lose it. He made Melbourne by way of the Cape of Good Hope in seventy-eight days; and back by Cape Horn in seventy six, well inside his self-imposed time limit. Legend has it that while in Melbourne, Forbes took no chances in losing his experienced crew to the lure of the goldfields, having them clapped into irons by the local authorities on grounds of insubordination.

Some detractors claim that it was 'Bully' Forbes who made *Marco Polo* run so fast, but other masters sailed her with almost as much success. She was advertised as the fastest ship in the world, and she was, once logging 428 miles in one day.

For thirty years she sailed the seas, until one day onlookers at Cavendish Beach, Prince Edward Island, watched helplessly as she sailed right onto a reef in a storm, and started to break up. The *Marco Polo* had been leaking like a sieve, and in a desperate attempt to save his crew — and himself no doubt — the captain had purposely run her aground.

The fame of this great ship brought a flood of orders to the Smith shipyard, but try as they may, they were never able to match her for speed. One has to wonder how often James Smith must have been tempted to let one of his new launchings go rocketing across the creek to the nearest mud bank in the hope that he might duplicate the 'hog' in *Marco Polo*'s hull.

While the shipbuilding trade flourished in the Bay of Fundy, a family of German descent were taking over trade on the North Shore. Three brothers, Joseph, Henry, and John Cunard were sent by older brother Samuel to open up business in the area, while he remained in Halifax.

At six feet, over two hundred pounds (90 kg.), twenty-two-year-old Joseph, was a man of boundless ambition. He took over leadership and in no time had control of the business. Ships were soon pouring out of yards at Bathurst, Chatham, Richibucto, and Kouchibouguac. Other concerns sprang up all over the region: saw mills, brickyards, fish warehouses, and stores.

However, Joseph did not have everything his own way, having an ongoing feud with Alexander Rankine, a competitor, that came to all-out war at times. Rankine held sway on the Miramichi's north shore from Newcastle while the Cunards ruled the south shore from Chatham. Still, business was booming, and everywhere he went he was greeted like visiting royalty by his subjects.

No question! This was the golden age of the Miramichi. As far back as 1819 almost three hundred ships had loaded up at the Miramichi ports, and five years later they actually surpassed Saint John's figures for the quantities of lumber shipped out. The boundless wealth of the hinterland's forests was being squandered with the same enthusiasm that the previous generation had cleaned out the St. John valley. Meanwhile life in the Miramichi was about as exuberant as frontier towns in the Wild West, or gold rush towns in the Yukon. A mix of sailors with time on their hands and Irish immigrants, who could usually find the time, kept the local authorities with no time on their hands at all. Throwing the celebrants into jail just seemed to concentrate the problem, and eventually a detachment of the 74th Regiment was sent to put a lid on things. They were there for six years and would doubtless have been there longer had it not been for the Great Fire of the Miramichi.

On October 7th 1825 a massive forest fire swept along the north shore of the river devastating Newcastle and Douglastown with the loss of one hundred and sixty lives. Two hundred buildings burned in Newcastle and a further hundred and fifty in outlying areas. Those were official figures, but setting a figure for the area of forest destroyed is not so easy. One has to realize that this part of New Brunswick had no more than a nodding acquaintance with the rest of the province. It had been connected, and only recently by road, and what a road it was. One hundred and fifty unpopulated miles (250km) of rivers, bogs, swamps, high ridges, cliffs and endless mud from Fredericton. The Miramichi was like a bad dream to visit, consequently it was much easier to accept hearsay as gospel, than to make personal evaluations, so the Great Fire spawned legends instantaneously – especially in its scope. It had been a very dry summer and there had been fires all over the place, and doubtless some of these got lumped in with the main event. Nonetheless figures of six thousand square miles, are almost certainly wild exaggerations, probably six hundred would be closer – still a major fire and much more costly in human life than the subsequent fire in Saint John.

Whatever else the fire might have done to the area, it really calmed the place down. Many of the population turned to agriculture for a livelihood, some left for the United States, and the Cunards turned their eyes northwards to the Nepisiguit and the Upsalquitch. It was then, in 1826 that the old French settlement of St.Peter's became Bathurst, and Joseph's empire spread.

He should have seen trouble looming while visiting England with big brother Sam. Sam was there to finalize a contract to carry the transatlantic mail on two steamships.

In 1848 it was suddenly all over for Joseph Cunard whose drastically over-extended credit was withdrawn. Overnight he was bankrupt. The crowds that had cheered his progress as he rode through Chatham, now jobless, hurled abuse at him.

Sam did better; the Cunard Line went on to become the most prestigious shipping line in the world.

By the 1880s the boom was over. The sleek wooden ships with their sails reaching for the winds, were being replaced by steel hulls powered by steam. They were a lot dirtier but they were a lot more reliable and, in general, faster. Speed was now the all-consuming passion. By the turn of the century only a few small yards limped along.

Apart from a flurry of activity during the First World War, shipbuilding virtually died in the Province of New Brunswick, until the construction of the dry dock in Courtenay Bay in 1923. Even then, except during World War Two, the industry was of secondary importance until purchased by the Irving family in the 1950s.

Eight

✧

The War of 1812

If the English had misjudged the strength and determination of their American colonies in 1775, the leaders of the new republic were no better at gauging the strength of the new nation that was taking shape to their north.

The war that broke out in North America was only a sideshow to the main event that raged across Europe, as Napoleon led his revolutionary army against the established regimes. Nevertheless President Jefferson saw his opportunity to tidy up the map of North America, and declared war on Britain, hoping that she would be too busy to pay much attention. Jefferson evidently felt that Canada was there for the taking, and expected little by way of resistance.

Indeed Jefferson could be excused a measure of over confidence. There was an air of defeatism throughout Canada that did not bode well for a strong defence, but the second generation Loyalists — even some of their ageing fathers — were quick to answer the call to arms. Of all people, the Loyalists understood the choices that they would face with an American takeover. They could drop everything that they had rebuilt and take flight again, or they could stay and face whatever abuse might be heaped upon them. It was this factor that brought most of them to the flag. The native population, and the French

Canadians also found reasons to resist the invasion of republicanism. Loyalty to Britain was a secondary factor.

When General Isaac Brock and Tecumseh took Detroit, and an American invasion was repelled at Queenston Heights, Ontario, everyone took heart. The war was inconclusive, both sides having their successes and failures over the two-year period. It was this inconclusiveness that finally guaranteed Canada's destiny as a separate nation.

At first, during the War of 1812, the inhabitants of New Brunswick lived an anxious existence, feeling rather vulnerable in their east coast isolation. However as it transpired there was very little fighting in the region, and thousands of young men left to lend a hand in Upper Canada.

Meanwhile back in the Maritimes privateering was a growth industry; no less than thirty vessels were involved. Certainly the most successful at the game was the *Liverpool Packet* which was credited with fifty prizes, despite being captured at one point by the Americans — who used her for the same purposes. However the *Packet* was recaptured and was still cutting a swath through American shipping, under Captain Caleb Seeley, when the war came to a close. The *Sir John Sherbrooke* also had a remarkable record, taking nineteen prizes in one three-month period.

Between the privateers and the Royal Navy press-gangs, which plagued the whole coastal area, regular merchant ships had difficulty maintaining crews. Some owners found it necessary to try solving the problem by urging sailors and militiamen to desert! Commerce must have its way.

New Brunswicker's nerves soon settled down when they found, to their great relief, that their New England neighbours were far more interested in trading with them than fighting them. State militias, which had trouble mobilizing their manpower in any event, refused to invade Canada. New England merchants and farmers felt quite comfortable selling supplies to British garrisons.

The people of St. Stephen, N.B., and Calais, Maine, have never had much difficulty living with their border, and there were times when their casual attitude tried the patience of officialdom. One such case was when a random check of the garrison at St. Stephen, showed a complete, and unaccounted for, lack of gunpowder. Records clearly indicated that an ample stock had been issued — no fighting had been reported. Where was it? It was finally confessed that they had lent it all to the Americans, who had not had enough of their own to celebrate the Fourth of July.

The American government was just as happy when the war ended. They were more sure of themselves now, and starting to see the wisdom of burying the hatchet with Britain. After all they spoke the same language, and still had an essential Englishness in their culture. Their love affair with revolution and republicanism, was now tainted with revulsion at the happenings in France. They had been delighted to see their new allies throw off the bindings of their monarchy, but had been shaken by the bloodbath that followed, and their return to tyranny under a different name. Perhaps the old British institutions could be worse.

The War of 1812 left New Brunswick with little more tangible than the Martello tower in West Saint John and the Blockhouse in St. Andrew's, to mark its passing. In terms of historic significance, however, it was the 'final word' in the American Revolution, and the Americans would never invade Canada again.

Nine

✧

More About Boundaries

As we have already seen, boundaries around the Maritimes have always been something of a state of mind. For instance, at different times the term Nova Scotia could refer to the land that resembles a collapsed balloon, leaning towards the southeast, at the tip of the Acadian Peninsula; or it could refer to the whole Peninsula comprised of present-day Nova Scotia, New Brunswick, and eastern Maine. At the times the French were in power, the same held true of Acadia. In fact the boundaries tended to be wherever those holding the political whip hand at the time, felt they should be. This haphazard way of doing business took a sharp turn to the formal, after the British had lost the Revolutionary War, and their loyal supporters had set up shop in New Brunswick, and Nova Scotia. Now the frontier between New Brunswick and Maine, became a bone of contention for the next fifty years or so.

The draughtsmen at the Treaty of Versailles in 1782 were characteristically vague in laying down the boundary line. Up to that time, the whole area was so wild and sparsely settled that it could not have mattered less where the line actually was, but now that separate countries were involved, it was necessary to be specific.

The best they could do was to designate a line which was supposed to follow the St., Croix River to its source, and from thence head north in a beeline to a range of hills to the south of the St. Lawrence. All this explanation sounds clear enough, and would have been, had there been any consensus on which actually was the St. Croix River. The Americans held that it was the river that runs into the Bay of Fundy at St. George: the Maguagadavic River. On the other hand the British held with equal conviction that it was the most westerly river to flow into Passamaquoddy Bay. The problem was partially solved when remnants of Des Monts' original settlement were found, and the Scoodic River, as it had been known, was renamed the St. Croix.

Unfortunately, the St. Croix is what the Malecites disarmingly call a 'difficult' river. This means that long stretches of it are given up to falls, rapids, ledges, and anything else that can make river travel unpleasant. For this reason upstream navigation was more of an adventure than most wanted to bother with. Consequently, nobody took the time to find the river's source; much less line it up with some obscure line of hills far to the north in Quebec. In fact nobody really cared much about it, until the inevitable happened. American lumbermen started running into Canadian lumbermen around the headwaters of the western tributaries of the St. John. It speaks volumes for the forest management practices of the day that, even back in the 1820s and 1830s, they were having to range that far back in the bush to find good lumber. Needless to say friction quickly developed between the competing lumbermen.

In the far northwest corner of New Brunswick, where its boundaries meet those of Quebec and Maine, lies an area long known as the 'Republic of Madawaska'. French Canadians filtering down from Quebec, Acadians back pedalling up the St. John River Valley, and Anglo-Saxons come to work in the lumber trade, mixed to make up a society that has always tended to make its own rules. Life has a flair in Madawaska that is hard to find elsewhere. Like St. Stephen/Calais the international boundary between Edmundston and the town of Madawaska is largely an illusion as far as the locals are concerned. The region's biggest employer, the huge Fraser paper mill, itself straddles the border. It was inevitable that some of the more colourful disputes should surface in this area.

In 1827, a man named James Baker came from Baie Chaleur, where he had been working, to Baker Brook a few miles to the west of Edmundston. James had come to claim the inheritance of his brother who had settled the property a decade earlier. The dead man, who had presumably given his name to the place, probably did not know it, but in leaving his property to James, he was going to keep the neighbourhood hopping for a while.

It is hard to say what point, if any, Baker was trying to make by flying the American flag on his property, but in doing so he certainly raised the hackles of the local magistrate, who ordered him to take the offending flag down. Two very stubborn men had met head on. Baker was finally arrested and taken off to Fredericton to stand trial. Considering that this exercise involved a round trip of over three hundred miles (480 km.), it shows that, even after fifty years, the flying of a flag could be a very sensitive issue.

At trial Baker's case lost a lot of its steam when it came out that he had once had recourse to a New Brunswick lawyer; had had his land surveyed by a New Brunswick surveyor; and like any prudent farmer had taken advantage of a provincial grant, offered for growing grain on new land. He was fined £25 and told to go home and behave himself.

Four years later Baker made the news in the local papers once more.

The State of Maine, still unhappy with the way that the border had been laid out, sent a team of 'surveyors' to check out the country north of Grand Falls. Surveyors they may or may not have been, but agitators they certainly were, directing most of their energies to stir up local folk in an attempt to persuade them to accept the jurisdiction of Maine. Authorities warned the people not to take part in the election that the 'surveyors' were trying to organize. Feelings ran high, amid sporadic violence, and the same authorities showed a strong presence at all meetings. It all finally settled down, but not before arrest warrants were issued to Baker for his part in what became known variously as the "Aroostook," or "Pork and Beans War."

Even the arrest managed to have an air of comedy about it. When the arresting officers arrived at the Baker farm, they found that Mrs. Baker had been left to answer the door, while her husband attended to "urgent business elsewhere." He eventually came out of the woods when all the hue and cry had died down, and any further action would have been just too much trouble.

As if "The Pork and Beans War" had not provided the border with enough bad comedy, there was more to come.

In 1839, a group with enough sense of destiny to call themselves the 'Maine Patriots' recruited a small army from among the people of Bangor, Old Town, and Lincoln. Marching resolutely into the disputed Aroostook River territory, they were determined to take prisoner any British subjects found taking American lumber.

However, the New Brunswick woodsmen had different thoughts. Hearing of the Patriots' advance, they ran off to Woodstock and armed themselves to the teeth. When the two sides confronted each other the Patriots found themselves badly outgunned, and it was the New Brunswickers that were taking the prisoners. This outcome was not in the script at all and the furious Patriots — what was left of them — scampered off to Houlton, demanding arms from the fort's commandant. He very wisely declined. The Maine men gathered another force together, intending to march on Fredericton, to gain release of their friends, but the matter was ultimately settled diplomatically.

The incident may have had all the inconclusiveness that seems to be so characteristic of Canadian/American relations, but it did lead to the final settlement of the dispute — a mere sixty years after it became an issue.

It was finally left to Daniel Webster, and Lord Ashburton to negotiate a binding agreement in 1842. Lord Ashburton was successful in retaining the absolute minimum amount of New Brunswick's claim. If anyone asked him about the great slice of northern Maine that almost isolated the province from the rest of Canada, he would shrug and pronounce it worthless anyway. The truth of the matter was more likely that, the less friction that existed between the United States and Britain, the happier things were in London.

On one point New Brunswick and Nova Scotia were adamant. The Bay of Fundy had always been a 'British sea,' and should remain so. The border was fixed from headland to headland, rather than following a three mile limit round the coast.

Ten

❦

The Irish

If it could be said that the nineteenth century belonged to New Brunswick, it most certainly could not be said of Ireland. For eight hundred years Ireland had been wracked by internal strife between petty princes, or ground down by English oppression. In either case the poor hovered between insurrection and starvation. The lot of the Irish peasant was at best tenuous, and when blight struck the potato crop in 1845, it spelled catastrophe.

Today, it is hard to believe that a potato crop could be pivotal to the survival of a European country, but the potato was the staple that kept the poorer Irish alive. As the blight spread, and the word spread, the countryside was seized by panic. The exodus began.

The first Irish to come to New Brunswick were not refugees from the potato famine — some may well have come as many as three centuries earlier. When the fishermen from northwest France touched on New Brunswick's shores in the sixteenth century, there was quite heavy trading between them and the people of southeast Ireland. It is very likely that there were men of Wexford and Waterford among them when they fished in Maritime waters.

Long before the flood of emigrants that would flee Ireland in the 1840s and 1850s, a relatively large number, overwhelmed by the hardships of their native land, decided to see if life was that bad everywhere. After the Duke of Wellington had put Napoleon down for good at Waterloo in 1815, disbanded Irish soldiers, returned to grim conditions in the homeland. The end of a major conflict often brings with it a hesitation in the economy. The homecoming soldiers and sailors found no work, and starvation was staring them in the face.

About thirteen thousand of them boarded ships to Halifax; from here many found their way to the Miramichi, and went to work in the lumber trade. These were the fortunate ones who survived the Atlantic crossing as human ballast for lumber ships returning empty from Britain to the Maritimes. Conditions on some of these ships was said to be worse than on slavers, and the immigrants arrived in terrible physical condition. Someone should have been paying attention — the lessons to be learned would have stood the authorities in good stead thirty years down the road, when the problem would return with a vengeance.

Again and again and again the dreaded blight struck the potato crop, and starvation held the Irish by the throat. With famine came all the usual famine-related disorders: typhus, dysentery, and scurvy. Efforts to set up temporary hospitals were well meaning but ineffectual. The Irish started flooding into Britain's drastically overcrowded industrial cities, adding to the abject poverty and disease already affecting the lower-class urban dwellers.

Some help may have been forthcoming from British Prime Minister Robert Peel. Peel tried hard for the repeal of the Corn Laws, which effectively barred the import of foreign grain to the British Isles. His party was split on the issue; nevertheless, he was eventually able to have the laws repealed, before he was forced to resign. It was much too late — it would be another three years before Canadian grain could be moved to Britain. Meanwhile supply remained short, and prices far beyond the reach of ordinary folk. The fates of three million starving Irish, and one hundred and fifty thousand highland Scots were sealed. It was emigrate or starve to death.

In 1847, 258,000 Irish left British and Irish ports; 143,000 left for the United States; 115,000 for British North America. About 17,000 of these last, came to New Brunswick, some through the Miramichi, but mainly through the port of St. John.

During the decade, the population of Ireland fell by three million. Many went to Britain, one million starved, and one million fled to face the horrors of the sea voyage, and the quarantine stations of Grosse Isle at Quebec, and Partridge Island, outside Saint John. A great many of these poor people were at death's door before they even left Irish shores. Gross overcrowding coupled with under-rationing, in filthy conditions made the spread of disease inevitable.

Officials in Saint John were warned that immigrants were coming their way, and from past experience they knew that they should expect a certain amount of sickness and poverty. Nevertheless they were in no way prepared for the actuality. Moses Perley, grandson of the pioneer of settlement on the St. John, was the government Emigration Officer in Saint John. He must have had misgivings, or better information than most, because in February 1847, he started agitating for improved facilities at the quarantine station on Partridge Island. There were only two existing fever sheds, which could accommodate no more than two hundred patients — woefully inadequate quarters. Ships started to arrive before the work could be carried out.

The first ship, the *Midas*, arrived at Partridge Island on May 5th with 163 passengers aboard; ten had died at sea, and others were sick with the fever. After the Midas there were a number of uneventful arrivals and officials started to breathe a little easier. Then on May 16th the *Aldebaran*, sailing out of Sligo on Ireland's impoverished northwest coast, arrived with 418 passengers. Further enquiries showed that at least 36 had died on the crossing, and 105 were sick on arrival — 80 died later in quarantine. A deadly pattern had been established. The nightmare had started.

By early June the facilities on Partridge Island were stretched beyond their limits. Twenty-five hundred souls were now in quarantine, with many more still waiting on board their ships among the dead and dying. The airless holds below decks added greatly to the rate of infection among those previously untouched. While at sea, the winds and the movement of the ships contributed to at least some change of air. Lying at anchor the holds became fetid hells.

On the island conditions were appalling, with the overflow from the sheds being lodged in makeshift tents. Some, understandably reluctant carpenters were enticed to build two more shelters. They helped but much more was needed. In fact, regardless of what was built there, the island itself, was proving to be totally inadequate to its task. It is not a large island — not much more than thirty acres (12 ha.), and the soil is rocky and sparse.

Burials were now taking place at a pace that could not be kept up with. The island's scant covering meant that bodies were buried with a mere scattering of soil over them. The smell of rotting corpses hung over the desperate community, adding to the health hazards and general misery of the immigrants.

The calamity produced its heroes.

By early June, the district Health Officer, Dr. George Harding who was swamped with work; was joined by his brother Dr. William Harding, and Dr. James Patrick Collins. Both William and James soon caught the fever and Dr. Collins died of it at the age of twenty-three, Harding recovered. In July Dr. William Mitchell volunteered his services but was also brought down by the fever shortly after, leaving the seemingly indestructible George Harding alone again with the disaster at its peak.

Dr. George was on his last legs when another wave of cases struck in August; finally, he, too, fell sick. His brother William, barely recovered from the illness himself, stepped back into the gap as Health Officer, with a Dr. Wetmore as assistant. In September Dr. Wetmore was transferred to the emigrant hospital at the county almshouse on the east side of Courtenay Bay. At this stage, the extra facility was handling a monthly average of 540 patients.

These men and their assistants were truly heroic, and enough cannot be said for them. The need was drastic and they did their best to fill it. They were not doing it for the fees — there were none. They laid their lives at risk, day after day, and did what they could for the hapless immigrants. Less should be said for the officials who saw the problems coming, and did little or nothing to prepare for them, but that is hindsight.

The real villains of the piece were the ruling class of Ireland, who found that it was much cheaper to ship their starving tenants out than feed them. These were the people who allowed — even initiated — what amounted to a mid-nineteenth century exercise in 'ethnic cleansing', by forcing them to emigrate. Many were in a desperate state before they were herded onto unseaworthy vessels, commanded by a breed of master who often had a callous disregard for the welfare of his charges.

A furious Moses Perley brought charges against thirteen of these ship's masters for offenses under the Passengers Act and was successful in gaining thirteen convictions.

Of the 17,000 Irish that embarked from Liverpool or Irish ports; official figures show that 823 died in passage; 601 died on Partridge Island; 595 died at the almshouse; and 96 died on Middle Island in the Miramichi. Perley's own estimate of the number of deaths runs at 2,500. He may have been skeptical of the numbers of the deaths at sea, or felt that officialdom was trying to minimize the effects of its own shortcomings.

If some officials reacted to the human disaster that had fallen upon them, by fudging figures; others were outraged by the condition of the immigrants, and the people who had caused them to be shipped out from Ireland. Notable among the culprits was future Prime Minister, Lord Palmerston, who had taken time out from his efforts to suppress the slave trade, to force thousands of starving tenants off his Irish estates.

A Mr. Ferrie, Honourable Member of the Legislative Council, and Chairman of the Emigration Commission in Montreal, rattled off a blistering letter to the Rt. Honourable Earl Grey, Secretary of State for Colonial Affairs in London:

> When blamed on going aboard the Vessel, in which they sailed in such a state of debility and want, they gave for answer, that they were starving at home, and were induced to that step by being promised many advantages, which they never realized. For instance, there have been this year about one thousand persons shipped off by the agents of Lord Palmerston who not only offered them clothes, but they were assured that his Lordship had agent in Quebec to whom instructions had been given to pay all from £2 to £5 each family according to their numbers. On arrival however no agents of his Lordship were to be found; and they were then

thrown upon the bounty of the government here and the charitable donations of private individuals.[1]

Barely taking time to insert a period, Ferrie unleashes a further broadside of moral indignation:

> If his Lordship was aware of this most horrible and heartless conduct on the part of his Irish agents, and he one of the ministers of the Crown, I dare not say what he would deserve. But that charity, my Lord, which "thinketh no evil," would teach me to hope that a nobleman of England, high in the confidence of her Most Gracious Majesty, and sharing in the honourable administration of her Government, could not so far to forget that duty he owed God, his Sovereign and his country, but that it was the wanton and unauthorized act of unprincipled hirelings, in whose bosoms every principle of humanity and germ of mercy had become totally extinct.[2]

Later in his letter Ferrie, still firing shots at Palmerston, notes that a public meeting in Saint John had made a decision, "to return the decrepit, aged and naked children and women brought to that port;" to his lordship's estates in Sligo. He was not the only Irish landlord to lend his name to this atrocity; Lords De Vesci and Fitzwilliam; Major Mahon and Captain Wanderford, all did their share in swelling the flood from the southeast. It was cheaper to ship them than care for them. Interestingly, not all the names are English.

Twenty-five years later the Irish population of New Brunswick stood at a hefty 100,000 out of a total population of 285,000; their impact on society must have been significant.

The Irish brought a great deal of their old inter-faith baggage with them. Surprisingly over half of those who came to the province at that time were Protestant, but this was not a situation that would last. Each religion seemed to pick its own turf. The Protestants predominated in the southwest corner of the province — in the counties of King's, Queen's, Charlotte, York, and Carleton. The Roman Catholics dominated in Saint John City and County; in the Miramichi; and anywhere the French Catholic population had become established. Rivalry between the two groups were not always friendly and clashes were frequent on the Glorious Twelfth of July, when a local 'King Billy', astride a white horse would lead the local Protestants in a parade to commemorate William of Orange's victory at the River Boyne.

One of the worst clashes occurred in Saint John in 1849, when a crowd of Orangemen provoked the overwhelmingly Catholic population of the York Point district, by parading through the area. Rocks and other missiles were thrown at the marchers, and warning shots were fired in retaliation. At Indiantown, in the city's north end, the Orangemen were reinforced by others, joining them from upriver. With their ranks expanded to six hundred well armed men, they set out on the return trip. Ignoring pressures to skirt the Catholic neighbourhood the marchers set forth once more into York Point — the area upstream from present day Market Slip. Again the air was thick with projectiles, and this time the Protestants counterattacked with guns blazing. Shots were exchanged and moments later a dozen lay dead and as many wounded. Sixty soldiers brought up from Lower Cove, seemed content to wait until the carnage was over — they then dispersed the crowd.

This event was not the end of inter-faith frictions between Irish Catholics and Protestants — they would endure for another hundred years; but its very violence forced the more responsible elements on either side to face up to the problem. The St. Patrick's Day Society in Saint John, deserves credit for putting all that nonsense in the past where it rightly belongs.

They brought the two sides together by rotating the presidency between 'Orange' and 'Green' members. The Protestant Irish population became less well defined over the years, as intermarriage between Protestants of English and Scottish backgrounds became commonplace.

The majority of the great influx of Irish to reach the province in the late 1840s, sooner or later moved on to Boston or New York. Most had intended to move in the first place, but had come to Canadian ports because the passage was cheaper, and restrictions on immigration much easier than in the United States, where their reception was cool.

For many, their memories of New Brunswick, could not have been happy ones.

Eleven

༄

Roadways, Railways and Waterways

Now that the North Atlantic coastline from Boston to Washington is essentially one big city, it is hard to conceive that, not much longer than two hundred years ago, New Brunswick, an area the size of Connecticut, Massachusetts, Vermont, and Rhode Island, had no roads. The fact of the matter is that when Lt. Governor Thomas Carleton, in Saint John, went to visit his ailing brother, Governor Guy in Quebec City, during the winter of 1788, he had to follow the time-honoured route over the river ice and through the woods. It was a nine-day trek for the Lt. Governor, eating on the march and sleeping in tents. A hot bath must have ranked high on his list of things to do when he reached Quebec.

Two hundred years after discovery by the Europeans the ways of getting about were still by canoe in summer, and by snowshoe in winter; no one planned trips for the spring.

It was not until the arrival of the Loyalists, who contributed towards roadbuilding in exchange for rights to buy property along the roads, that any real work was done. The first contact by road from Quebec, reached tentatively over the Gaspé, by way of the Matapedia Valley to the Restigouche. A second route, to the Madawaska by way of Lake Temiscouata, did not happen until the 1840s.

With Loyalists settling all over the place, roads started to reach out from one community to the next. Saint John to the east; Shediac to the Miramichi; the Miramichi to Bathurst and on to Campbellton on the Restigouche River. In an early 'roads to resources' program, roads followed such rivers as the St. Croix, to help exploit the forests.

Right after the War of 1812, technology came to the St. John River with the launching of the *General Smyth*. The *Smyth* was the first of many steamboats to ply the river. They ran as far upstream as Woodstock — smaller versions ventured to Grand Falls — until the old *Purdy* was finally decommissioned in 1946.

Not everyone was impressed by the newfangled steam run boats. A Hampstead farmer named William Peters, could recognize the sound principles of the paddle wheel as a means of propulsion, but figured — rightly — that the steam boiler was quirky at best, and lethal at worst. Therefore he thought of combining the principles of the paddle wheel with a more conventional form of horsepower. He designed and built a craft one hundred feet long, with a twelve armed capstan amidships. To each of these he harnessed a horse, and on the command "Giddy Up' the twelve horses would plod around the capstan, which was connected to the paddle wheels by a system of gears.

On her maiden run the horseboat — as it became known — set off into the current and was not doing too badly, until one of the onlookers hollered "Whoa"! This procedure characterized every attempt Peters made to test his idea. Every time the boat got going there would be a spirited "Whoa"! from the delighted crowd and the horses would gratefully grind to a halt. Peters was obliged to shelve his project and the horseboat finished its life as a houseboat for lumberjacks on Grand Lake.

William Peters, notwithstanding, rapid communication was starting to become a reality. When Saint John established a telegraph link with Boston, the New York press saw a means of speeding up the transmission of news. Representatives would meet the mail ships at Halifax, and relay the news to Digby, in eight hours, by means of a 'pony express'. From Digby it was sailed across the Bay of Fundy to Saint John by ferry, and the telegraph did the rest. It was thus possible to have the morning news in Halifax as evening news in New York. It was a good scheme but it did not last long — some top-flight horsemen were put out of work, and the horses out to pasture, by a telegraph link from Saint John to Halifax.

Travel was still a long way from carefree. The roads were like goat tracks by today's standards. Only the busiest of thoroughfares were planked and one could not count on all boggy sections being 'corduroyed' — a technique of laying tree trunks side by side. Ironically, the best time for a warmly dressed traveller to move about was in winter. The ground was frozen, the outlines of rocks and stumps softened by layers of snow, and the coach ran smoothly on runners. In those days, the one hundred and fifty mile (200 km) run from Saint John to Amherst took three days. Springtime was another matter.

The difficulties of building roads in New Brunswick were boundless. There were hardly any old trails to follow, and the land was as wild as anywhere. The country may not have been mountainous, but it was extremely hilly, and crisscrossed by lakes, bogs, and fast-flowing streams and rivers. Low population density also created problems. Building roads over long distances made the per capita cost high, and funds for maintenance low.

Naturally many of the difficulties in roadbuilding applied equally to building railroads. There were also technical problems in trying to adapt an essentially British technology to

Canadian conditions, particularly the vast distances and the winter — a built-in problem for any project in Canada.

Since the invention, and rapid development of the steam engine in England, railroad fever had swept North America, and Maritimers were determined to have one of their own. In what might have been a look into the crystal ball of Business/ Government relations, railway construction in Canada instantly became a quicksand for public money. As often as not the motives for building a line, revolved as much around filling pockets with government grants as the desire to connect one point in the country to another.

The railways became the great Canadian 'cash cow,' begging to be milked by politicians and promoters alike. There were always gentle hands at the udder, ensuring that it never got too full.

The first railway project to stir the blood of Maritimers was the Intercolonial Railway, which proposed to link Halifax with Quebec City by way of the North Shore of New Brunswick. The object was to provide the St. Lawrence and Great Lake region with access to the Atlantic during winter, while the waterway was clogged by ice. At the same time it would allow the east coast to share in the development of the interior, which was growing in leaps and bounds.

The route would bypass Saint John and Fredericton, thus being of little use to New Brunswickers, apart from those who lived in the sparsely settled east and northeast — or anyone fortunate enough to own land along the way. Saint John as the industrial centre for the east, with sea links to American markets, saw her efforts to secure a connecting line with Shediac shot down by the Legislative Council.

It was assumed that the Government in London would help finance the Intercolonial, but British investors were becoming a little 'gun shy' on railway projects in North America. In mid 1850 they turned the project down.

The door was now left open for the European and North American Railway, the brainchild of a John Poor of Bangor, Maine. As the name of the railway would imply, Poor was a man of vision. His vision, and it seemed like a good one, was to run a line from Portland, Maine to Quebec City with connections running south. Furthermore he proposed to build another line eastward through southern New Brunswick, all the way to Halifax. In doing so the E. and N.A.R. stood to knock eight hundred miles (1,300 km) off the sea voyage to northern Europe — with ferry connections to St. John's Newfoundland, a thousand.

When London changed its mind again and approved the financing of the Intercolonial, it looked as though New Brunswickers' dreams were finally being answered, and that they were going to have the best of both worlds. It was not to be. The British flip-flopped again and shelved plans for the I.C.R. indefinitely. John Poors financing dissipated; New Brunswick was left sitting between two chairs. Actually a large section of the E. and N.A.R. was built eventually and by 1869 stretched from Shediac via Saint John to Vanceboro, Maine.

When the I.C.R. did finally arrive it was only at the insistence of Nova Scotia, as a condition for joining confederation. As a project it was not without its wrinkles, quickly becoming a bottomless pit for government funds, as politicians and their friends competed for elbow room around the trough.

The building of the I.C.R. had a positive effect upon a small community in the southeast of the province. A 'bend on the Petitcodiac River' became Moncton — an important transportation axis for road and rail as Saint John forged its links with Intercolonial traffic.

Though relatively small in population New Brunswick was well on its way to being an industrial society. Roads and railways make the world smaller in one sense, but they can make it much bigger too. Those who lived in out of the way places, could now make contact with folks down the road. A farmer could now move his produce to another town; on the other hand, a furniture maker might find that his previously captive clientele were now buying the odd stick of furniture somewhere down the line. Trade became more competitive; the road to domination by the big firm was being paved.

Shipbuilding was losing ground to other industry. Steamships with steel hulls were taking over from wooden sailing ships. The same people who had celebrated the arrival of the first steam locomotive in town, now watched in dismay as the same technology shifted all the shipbuilding to the heavy industrial centres like Belfast, the Clyde, and Tyneside. Actually the days of shipbuilding were already numbered in the Maritimes. The forests had been plundered clean and, incredible as it may seem, material was getting to be in short supply.

Despite the loss of this business, which devastated some areas — the Miramichi, for example — the overall economy continued to grow. The Intercolonial's shipping rates were highly competitive, and Maritime producers found ready buyers for their goods in central Canadian markets. The province continued to prosper.

With rates as low as fifty percent of their competitors the I.C.R. was still able to show a profit; so some sort of remedial action was inevitable. In 1919, the I.C.R. was engulfed by an emerging national system. It was renamed the Canadian National Railway; its head office was moved from Moncton to Toronto; and to the best of anyone's knowledge, it has never made money since.

The freight rates were increased to central Canadian levels immediately; and then again by a further forty percent to pay for the new system's mind-numbing debt load. The effect on New Brunswick's industry was ruinous.

In 1883, the Canadian Pacific opened their 'short line' that ran from Saint John, through northern Maine, to Montreal, thus giving the port of Saint John the theoretical advantage of being served by both national rail systems. In practice the two giants viewed competition as a very nasty word, and it never made the slightest difference. Until recently it was possible to board a passenger train in the evening in Saint John, and wake up refreshed in Montreal, early next morning. How refreshed depended upon the type of accommodation paid for and the amount of time spent in the club car. Now there is no more C.P. in the Maritimes, The train ride to Montreal now involves a hundred mile (160 km) bus trip to Moncton from whence the weary traveller can connect with CN's line to Montreal. C.P. said they never made any money either. Much of the 'short line' has recently been bought by the Irving group, who are operating it under the name of the Southern New Brunswick Railway, which will make money.

Twelve

❦

Confederation

When Guy Carleton — now Lord Dorchester — returned to Canada in 1786, he was not only the King's chief representative; he was the first to hold power over Upper and Lower Canada, and the territory composed of New Brunswick, Nova Scotia, St. John's Island, and Ile Royale (now Prince Edward Island, and Cape Breton Island respectively). This would be the first faltering step into the maze of confederation.

Governor Parr's shortcomings were becoming obvious even to London; so in 1784, it was mainly for bureaucratic reasons that New Brunswick and Cape Breton were split away from the territory that had finally established itself as Nova Scotia in 1713. Cape Breton would rejoin Nova Scotia in 1820, and from thenceforth the Maritimes would take their present form. Each of the three resulting provinces sported its own government, its own legislature and its own flourishing civil service. It still took them the better part of a century to form the Dominion of Canada.

In 1837, half-hearted rebellions broke out in both Upper and Lower Canada (Ontario and Quebec). The outbreaks were dealt with easily enough, but put Britain on notice that there were urgent problems that needed to be straightened out. Lord Durham was sent out as governor to do what he could.

Confederation

Two more diverse societies than heavily French Lower Canada, and solidly Anglo-Saxon Upper Canada, would be hard to find; but Durham was undeterred. In essence he followed the wishes of the Montreal merchants who wanted to create a single trading area by uniting the two. It was also felt privately that unification would speed up the assimilation of the French.

The first objective met with limited success, the second none at all, but that is not to say that the Act of Union of 1840 was a failure. It was far from it. With each province having forty seats in the new legislature, and by switching the capital back and forth between Montreal and Kingston every three years, sensitivities were calmed. The new unit's divisions, Canada East and Canada West, were a compromise, but nonetheless a great step in the right direction. It was now only a matter of time before pressure would be brought to bear on the eastern colonies to join in.

In 1871 census figures show that the population of New Brunswick was just under 300,000; Nova Scotia just under 400,000; Prince Edward Island under 100,000; about one fifth of the overall Canadian tally. Despite these facts the Maritimes were in no hurry to oblige. Each of the three governors were quite comfortable with the power that they wielded, no matter how few people they actually wielded power over. Further unification was unlikely until they changed their attitudes.

Generally speaking, attitude changes only come with prompting; and by the 1860s there were compelling reasons to take a second look, but first...

In September 1864, hearing that the three colonies were meeting at Charlottetown, to discuss Maritime Union — they still do sometimes — the two Canadas asked if they could join in. The Canadians were well prepared when they arrived, and met with a surprisingly eager audience. The Maritimers had exhausted all the usual topics of Maritime unity, and were starting to think along broader lines as road, rail and sea travel became part of their everyday lives. When MacDonald of Ontario, and Cartier of Quebec, pointed out that the rapid development of the American west, would pose a threat to the undeveloped Canadian west, their own vulnerability became more apparent. Furthermore the wrapping up of the American Civil War added more urgency. Britain had taken sides with the Confederacy and was consequently open to reprisals from the victorious Unionists.

Further meetings were held in Halifax and Saint John; there was a great deal of partying and no dearth of speeches. They were having so much fun that they called a follow-up meeting for Quebec in October.

The strongest figure to emerge from the second conference was Quebec's George Etienne Cartier. Fearing that 'les Canadiens' could become completely engulfed by the unification process, Cartier held out for much wider powers than his Anglo ally might have wished for. Newfoundland attended these meetings for the first time.

When the leaders all returned to their respective legislatures, their proposals were met with mixed reactions. Canada West's assembly shot theirs through with a 54 to 8 vote. Canada East was a little tighter at 37 to 25. The proposals fared less well elsewhere. New Brunswick's Leonard Tilley was in favour of confederation, but had to face an election, which he lost. Prince Edward Island thought things were fine the way they were. Nova Scotia's Charles Tupper was for the plan but lost his backing with New Brunswick — his only link — out of the picture. Newfoundland was a non-starter, as links with the mother country were closer there and communication with London easier than it was with Upper Canada.

Strangely enough when help came it was from two completely unexpected quarters, that had absolutely no interest in Canadian unity whatsoever. To the contrary, in fact.

The United States was the first unwitting proponent of confederation when it revoked the Reciprocity Agreement of 1854. 'Reciprocity' was a kind of free trade agreement covering natural products. Natural products included lumber and fish, both major New Brunswick exports. The loss of preferential treatment would be a major blow. The termination of the agreement was on the grounds that the Confederates had been allowed to use Canadian soil for both land and naval attacks, and Washington was showing its displeasure. Since New Brunswick's natural trading area in New England was, to a large extent withdrawn, merchants were forced to look in other directions. The next nearest markets were Quebec and Ontario.

A more improbable impetus toward Confederation was the threatened incursions of the Fenians. The Fenian Brotherhood were a volatile broth of Irish soldiers disbanded from the Union Army of the United States. Their expressed objectives were clear enough, if thought provoking; they vowed to liberate Ireland by invading Canada.

One incursion at Fort Erie was sent packing. A second on the Vermont/Quebec border was rounded up by the Americans themselves. The third attempt involved some Fenians from Maine who sought to capture Campobello Island, of all places. None of these attempts were very threatening, but enough to remind New Brunswickers of their vulnerability from that direction.

Another election returned Tilley to power, and New Brunswick was now on side with Nova Scotia. If any further pressure was needed, Britain provided it. If trading woes and military threats played their parts in the influence of Maritime thought, Her Majesty's Government fell over themselves in their eagerness to tidy up her remaining North American possessions. The last thing either they or their investors wanted was to invest their hard earned cash in was a string of little colonies. They much preferred the idea of a large monolithic country.

When the two Canadas, Nova Scotia, and New Brunswick met in London they were of one accord. Improvements had been made in the agreement, and the long dreamt of Intercolonial Railway, became reality as a prerequisite of the canny Tupper's signature on behalf of Nova Scotia.

Along with the Dominion of Canada the British North America Act was born in 1867. Prince Edward Island, lonely, joined the club in 1873. For Newfoundland it would be another eighty years.

Looking through his Bible after the signing, the deeply religious Tilley found both the title and the motto for the new nation.

Psalms 72:8. "he shall have Dominion from sea to sea"

Thirteen

❦

Post-Unity Depression
1867-1900

The British North America Act had hardly started to gather dust before an economic turndown struck the Maritimes. The recession did not only affect the Eastern part of Canada, it was world wide. That fact, however, did not stop many people laying the blame squarely at the feet of Confederation. Maritimers felt that they were poorly represented at the top of the country's bureaucratic food chain — they were; and they felt that they had been short-changed in cabinet representation; that feeling was true too. Prime Minister John A. MacDonald had quite naturally tended to award the top positions in both cabinet and civil service to people he knew, but it was not policy and it would change with time.

Ottawa was not responsible for this 'business correction' but presented itself as a handy lightning rod. It was felt particularly acutely in New Brunswick, because it coincided with a total collapse in wooden shipbuilding and fish exports to the West Indies and the United States.

In recent years the increased difficulty in selling ships abroad had led to many of them being taken over by local business. If you can't sell them, sail them. For a while Canada boasted the fourth biggest merchant navy in the world, and a major part of this fleet sailed out of Saint John. However, they were relegated to coastal trade because steel and steam had taken over the high seas.

Farming was the leading sector in the provincial economy by now, and this community was able to weather the recession better than most. Apart from the obvious fact that one is less likely to starve if one grows food, recent improvements in transportation had made movement of goods to nearby communities more practical, and even dairy products could be moved swiftly and safely.

Specialized farming started to appear in the province as early as the 1890s; dairy farming took over the Sussex area, midway between Saint John and Moncton. Farmers were quick to realize that something in the soil of the upper Saint John River Valley appealed to potatoes, and to this day they remain the predominant crop in the region.

Railway construction, ever a great gatherer of votes and filler of deep pockets, continued to blossom in the late nineteenth century. Fredericton was connected to the Miramichi, cutting through sparsely or totally unpopulated areas. Moncton as the regional rail centre, continued to flourish in an otherwise lacklustre world. Meanwhile travel between New Brunswick and Prince Edward Island had its challenges.

In 1873, when the Islanders had begrudgingly joined Confederation, they had done so on condition that Ottawa provide them with a transportation link to the mainland. The Federal Government acted upon this commitment with about the same enthusiasm as the Island had joined Confederation. The link showed up, ultimately in the form of the *Golden Light*. Whatever images its name was supposed to convey, the old bucket was certainly no ball of fire. She was an exhausted old, wooden-hulled St. Lawrence steamer, and on her best day, better known for time in repair than her clockwork schedules.

The fact of her wooden hull made winter crossings a bad bet. The ice-clogged straits between Cape Tormentine and Borden were no place for a wooden hull and alternate means of crossing had to be found. The alternative was not for the frail or the faint of heart. Wintertime travel became a nightmarish ordeal with 'passengers' hauling and pushing small boats fitted with runners across the ice and sailing across open patches of water. This mode of travel did not suit everyone, and matters were brought to a head when a sudden violent snowstorm forced a boatload of people to try to take shelter on the ice. The frostbitten group was finally rescued, but not before they had burnt the boat and all the mail for fuel.

This near tragedy, and in all likelihood the use of the mail for fuel, provoked such an uproar that the federal government were forced to look for a different and better solution. Sturdier, more reliable ships were put into service.

One suggestion raised at the time was the construction of a nine mile (15 km) tunnel connecting Cape Tormentine to the Island. This idea, or related ideas such as bridges, combined tunnels and bridges, and causeways, were to exercise minds on both sides of the Northumberland Strait for the next hundred years. However, for the time being, the Islanders had to settle for a spur of the ICR to Cape Tormentine.

The tunnel might have seemed like an ambitious scheme to serve some ninety thousand souls, but it was the age of grand designs, and perhaps less air-headed than the plan to build a railroad to carry ships across the Chignecto isthmus, between the Bay of Fundy and Northumberland Strait — a project that actually did get started.

What with the dwindling economy of the region, and the fact that Saint John was rapidly losing its eminence as one of Canada's leading cities, the Great Fire of 1877, could have been a death blow. There had been fires before — even some major ones — but this fire was of huge dimensions.

The fire broke out in a building on Smyth Street, in the North Slip area of York Point, mid-afternoon June 20th. Fuelled by the densely crowded frame buildings, and a gale blowing out of the northwest, the flames were out of control in no time. They leapfrogged across Market Slip through the masts and rigging of the ships moored there, surging towards the South End. Panic gripped the city as the firefighters were forced to back up before the flames, ever conscious of the blazes starting behind them, as the wind carried firebrands over their heads.

As usual, in times of stress, the fire produced its share of heroic deeds and 'Good Samaritans'; however, there were few of these among the city's carting community. The carters had a field day, charging as much as $50 a load to move victims' belongings from the path of the flames. They were not the only thieves as society's carrion pickers looted and robbed the desperate citizens.

King Square was crowded with people and their belongings piled up about them. When the jail was evacuated, two or three of the prisoners took advantage of the confusion to escape. Having done that, unable to find anywhere to go, they gave themselves up again.

When it was all over 40% of the city had burned; at least 18 had died; 1,600 houses were lost; 13,000 were homeless; about 20 ships were lost; the cost was placed at $27,000,000 of which only $7,000,000 was insured — causing a massive drain on local capital.

However, it was not all bad news. Federal money was brought in, and skilled workers shelved their plans to move

West or to New England, as the city tried to cope with the biggest building boom since the Loyalists landed. Federal funding was used to modernize the port. Accordingly, management of the facilities was assumed by Ottawa and one more bit of local control slipped away.

Textiles were a major industry in neighbouring New England, and now a number of Maritime centres, convinced that cotton mills were the road to prosperity, planned mills of their own. There had been a cotton mill in Saint John for some years, and it had survived the fire; others were built at Milltown — on the Maine border at St. Stephen; in Marysville on the St. John, opposite Fredericton; and in Moncton.

The industry was soon drastically overbuilt, and despite attempts at self regulation, the markets were simply unable to absorb all the production, and within a decade most had failed. Nevertheless these mills, though they may have failed as business ventures, had a lasting effect upon society. They needed plentiful labour and it had to be cheap. For the first time women were allowed to enter the labour market in numbers.

By the end of the century women had not progressed very far, but they were on the verge of making breakthroughs towards gender equality. They were still essentially chattels who could not own property under normal circumstances, or vote in elections; nor were they free to choose the type of work they wished to do. These facts were particularly true of the middle classes who, by convention, were not expected to work in factories or stores. A single woman could become a school teacher, as long as she remained single, but by and large, the middle-class woman who wanted more mental stimulation than reading poetry, playing piano, or overseeing domestic servants, was more or less restricted to joining organizations that spent their time doing good works.

Doing good works may seem trivial enough, but in fact, some of these women's groups became very powerful in influencing public opinion, and were to a very large extent responsible for the gradual growth of 'social conscience'.

One such organization was the Women's Christian Temperance Union, which had nothing to do with temperance, and everything to do with total prohibition. Even before Confederation, temperance — or rather prohibition — became an issue, under Tilley's mandate, and the province had actually flirted with it briefly at that time. The women who formed the backbone of the move towards sobriety and social values were the logical people to carry the banner. It was they who bore the brunt of the results of chronic alcoholism, and they who were the first victims of social injustice. It was they who had to cope with the lack of health care for their children, and the general indifference shown to the plight of their sex.

The temperance groups, who were overwhelmingly Anglo-Saxon and of the evangelical forms of Protestantism, were involved in areas other than temperance. One of their other interests centered on education, which they strongly felt should be non-sectarian and integrated. This contention brought them into headlong conflict with the Roman Catholics who held just as strongly that education should be sectarian and separate.

Eventually the first cracks in the egg shell started to appear. The daughters of the middle classes had already won the right to a certain amount of advanced education, and in 1872, Mount Allison University in Sackville, opened its doors to women. Thus a major barrier had been breached. In 1876, the women of New Brunswick were at last allowed to vote in municipal elections.

By Confederation, nothing much had changed in the Acadian community either. Their society had not changed much from the days before the Expulsion. It was almost as though their experiences had taught them that life was much easier if one kept the head down and stayed out of sight. The clergy were still very much in control, still bent on keeping their charges fixed into a rural existence. They gathered themselves behind the covered wagons of their enclave, which covered the northeast half of the province, and maintained a phenomenal birth rate. Their proportion of the population grew to nearly 18%; it would ultimately approach 40%.

Now in the final years of the century the Acadians started to move from under the influence of the priests and left the obscurity of one hundred and fifty years behind them. Improved education became an issue for them — a French speaking college, St. Joseph's, was opened at Memramcook. With education a new sense of cultural awareness developed. A French language newspaper appeared giving them a voice of their own. With a new flag — the French colours with a gold star top left — they forged themselves a new identity uniquely Acadian, Acadian as distinct from French-Canadian.

Progress was not made without incident. The Acadians were part of the Roman Catholic population which accounted for about a third of the overall provincial total. The Roman Catholics, as an entity, were locked into a major dispute with the Protestant majority on the subject of education, stoutly claiming their right to educate their children in their own way. There had been confrontations between the bishops and government on the issue, with no ground being given up by either side. When the bishops instructed their flocks not to pay their school taxes, they were only too happy to comply. The government reacted by seizing Catholic property wherever they could find it — including Saint John Bishop Sweeny's horse and carriage.

A group of Protestants in Caraquet, an overwhelmingly Catholic community, with more fervour than forethought, tried to replace the elected parish council with more compliant members. There was a riot; constables were called in to deal with it.

Some of the agitators had gathered at the house of Andre Albert, and hearing that the constables were on their way, went to hide in the attic. When the constables burst through the door a Constable Ramsay fired up through the trapdoor, and two others stormed up the ladder only to be thrust back. Someone fired back and a bullet ricocheted off Mme. Albert's stove. Two more men stormed the ladder and John Gifford dropped with a bullet in his head. Then everyone started firing blindly through the ceiling and Louis Mailloux fell mortally wounded. By now the trapped agitators had had enough and surrendered. Nine men were carted off to Bathurst in an open vehicle, in bitter cold, many being frostbitten on the way. They were charged with Ramsay's murder, but only one, Joseph Chiasson, was brought to trial. Chiasson was found guilty and sentenced to hang, but the verdict was overturned by the Supreme Court.

A compromise was eventually worked out which fell short of their aspirations but gave the Roman Catholics much of what they were seeking. For the Acadians it was a vital step in their long-standing resistance to assimilation.

Fourteen

❦

War at Home and Away
1900-1920

The new century dawned on New Brunswick like a foggy Fundy day. New Brunswickers peered anxiously into a misty future that promised to clear up — but might not.

On the surface the regional economy seemed reasonably buoyant, but there were underlying weaknesses. Bit by bit, Maritime business was becoming a branch office operation, with all the hazards of outside control. Effective control of the regional banks slipped away to central Canada, including the Royal, and the Bank of Nova Scotia, both to become giants in international banking. One of the last holdouts, the Bank of New Brunswick, was taken over by the Bank of Nova Scotia in 1913. The disappearance of the banks from the local scene contributed greatly to the flight of capital.

The railways continued to spread this way and that like ill-controlled children. The ICR which made some kind of sense was duplicated by a second link from Quebec to Moncton, giving shippers another choice, hardly justified by the volume of traffic. A further line was run down the St. John River Valley on a cost sharing basis with the federal government. Later Ottawa backed out of the adventure, citing the war effort as an excuse to change its mind, thus leaving the province saddled with a huge debt.

The years leading up to the First World War were marked by a growing militancy in labour. British immigrants steeped in a history of organized labour, and union organizers from Upper Canada and the United States were effective in transplanting their ideas in New Brunswick workers. The waterfront and construction trades unionized and so did the employees of the street railway system of Saint John.

The Saint John Street Railway was no shining example of labour/management relations, nor of company/public relations. Workers were forced to work ten hour days, seven days a week; service was poor and there was a stubborn resistance to upgrading the system.

The street railways were central in the new mobility of the working classes. Beyond being cheap transportation to work and shopping, they became an important part of their lives, stretching out into the suburbs and taking urban dwellers to picnic sites and social gatherings. Thus with both workers and public fed up with the company, the strike, when it came, received widespread support.

A march by union members had attracted a crowd of several thousand supporters to Market Square, and when a pair of streetcars, run by scab workers from Montreal clattered into the Square from Dock Street, they ran right into a rock storm. At that time the police force was in no way up to handling a crowd of that size, and in any event enjoyed about the same level of popularity as the street railway company. Mayor James Frink, unfazed, took the time honoured steps that Saint John mayors always took in times of crisis. He called for the militia and read the riot act to a silenced crowd. They had started to drift away when the incredible happened.

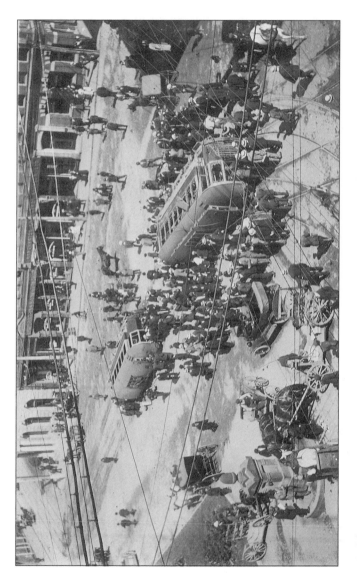

Herbert J. Blois **Street Car Strike, Saint John, New Brunswick**, 1914 silver print mounted on card
18.4 x 27.8 cm NBM Photograph Collection (X12493)

Who knows what tunes of glory were humming in the head of Lt. Hubert Stethem of the Royal Canadian Dragoons when he answered the call. Dismissing the riding class he had been instructing, he gathered about him six mounted troopers, and left Barrack Green in the South End for the scene of the action. Wheeling his formation in King Square, he brought them up in line abreast. Barely pausing to draw breath they drew their swords and charged down King Street at full gallop.

Astonishing as it may seem there were no deaths in the resulting chaos, and only a few wounded. These included two horses, and Lt. Stethem whose nose was cracked by a bottle; an eye blackened; and his scalp bloodied, before he and his bedraggled troop retreated up King Street in search of a better idea. The better idea came in the form of five hundred militiamen, who brought everything back to order, but not before the two streetcars were burned, and a great deal of storefront glass was broken. It was the mayor's third term — and his last.

The strike was settled quickly after all this, and the street railway system hung on tenaciously to both its franchise and its unpopularity until the city started paving over the tracks in the 1940s.

The outbreak of war in 1914, brought with it a mood of patriotism that was reflected in the relations between labour and management. For a few years there was virtual peace, but all that would go up in flames before the troops came marching home in 1918 and 1919.

Remote though it seemed, the war had a profound effect on New Brunswickers. In general they were loyal and proud members of the British Empire. Without waiting to be asked, many had answered the call for the Boer War, fifteen years earlier. What could be more remote than that? Authorities expected that the recruiting stations would be swamped. The actuality fell far enough short to be embarrassing. The percentage of eligible males presenting themselves for service fell far below the West and Ontario; it even fell below Nova Scotia. Mass rallies and parades, held all over the province drew enthusiastic crowds — but they had come to hear the music. Nevertheless thousands of men and women did leave their homes, full of hope and determination to ' bloody the Hun's nose'.

The lukewarm enlistment rate should not have been a great surprise in a community that was largely of Acadian or Irish descent; after all neither group could be said to owe deep affection for the British flag. And British flag it was, since the Canadian Army was an adjunct to the Imperial Army with limited autonomy. In fact many people of Acadian and Irish backgrounds, did volunteer to fight in the war, and oddly enough, although The Acadians voted in a solid block against conscription in 1917, their press and their clergy overwhelmingly endorsed the war effort. In all, about four thousand of them put on the uniform and headed for the front.

The Canadian Navy's start in 1880 might have been better. After bothering the British Government for long enough to provoke action, Ottawa finally won a commitment for a training ship. As the Admiralty looked around for a suitable vessel, someone must have mentioned the *Charybdis* — an ancient steam corvette limping her arthritic course homeward from the China Station. On her arrival in the U.K. she was fitted out with new boilers, (Ottawa was billed for them) and sent on her halting way across the Atlantic. Arriving in Saint John harbour *Charybdis* was tied up to the wharf — but not well enough. The crew barely had time to clamber onto the dock in search of the local highlife, before she broke loose from her mooring lines in a gale, and wandered about the harbour caroming from one ship to the next. Eventually she was corralled and returned to her proper berth, but she was not done yet. Two local men, calling on the ship, perhaps with damage claims, fell through the rotting gangplank, and drowned.

This was the last straw. She was towed back to Britain and returned to a reluctant Royal Navy, who had been congratulating themselves for having successfully ridded her from the fleet. The *Charybdis* became a thirty-year excuse for not starting a Canadian Navy. Any time the subject came up, people would shake their heads and mutter, "Remember the Charybdis."

By 1910 the government were able to put *Charybdis* behind them, and by 1914 the Royal Canadian Navy was sporting a brace of elderly cruisers discarded by the British Navy. The next four years would see substantial growth.

Good management and war seldom go hand in hand, but the First World War broke fresh ground for ineptitude. Equipped with twentieth century weaponry and nineteenth century minds, generals on both sides competed for the highest casualty lists.

Canadian troops did better than most, and in 1918 at the Battle of Vimy Ridge, it is said that Canada came of age. The Canadian Corps, which included the 26th. New Brunswick Battalion, had successfully resisted attempts by the British General Staff to spread them around among the British regiments; and had already impressed by holding firm at Ypres, while French and African Colonial troops had fled the first poisoned gas attack. Now they stormed and recaptured Vimy Ridge after all previous allied attempts had failed. 3,600 Canadians died that day. New Brunswickers were also in the front lines at Arras in 1917 and 1918; the Somme; the Hindenberg

Line; and Passchendaele where two Canadian Divisions knocked out seven smaller but very good German divisions. It was the Chief of the Kaiser's army General Paul von Hindenberg who noticed that a gathering of Canadian troops usually presaged an attack. He also knew why. The colonial troops were certainly no braver than their British counterparts, but coming from the forests and farms of the new world they were bigger and fitter than their cousins from the smoke-choked cities of the old world.

In an era when the glorification of war was as natural as the glorification of God, this war shook even the most hidebound patriot. As the casualty figures came in, and the numbers of dead and wounded started to climb, disillusionment set in. When all the figures were added up; of the 620,000 Canadians who served in the First World War, 60,000 died and 173,000 were wounded. Incidentally the last casualty of World War 1 was Jack Hickman of Dorchester who was killed by a stray bullet in 1919 during a riot by Canadian troops near Liverpool. The riot was caused by tempers boiling over at the authorities dragging their feet at repatriating the soldiers as more urgent needs for the shipping were found.

Disillusionment changed to revulsion as some of the stories of profiteering surfaced. It is almost a given fact that many of those who stay at home to tend the hearths, feel that as long as they are there they might as well tend to their pockets also. There were the usual stories of faulty equipment being sent out to fighting men and corruption proving more enriching than patriotism. One of the more flagrant cases was the 'Patriotic Potato Scandal'.

In 1914 the New Brunswick government had generously donated 100,000 bushels of potatoes to the war effort — not an inconsiderable gift in those days. Unfortunately it came to light later that a number of Tory supporters had taken the opportunity to make a fat profit out of shipping the gift to Europe.

As is normal, after a major conflagration, business that had been held aloft by the war effort overheating the economy, had skidded into a recession by the end of the decade. Workers who had held the line on wages during the war, as they worked in the shipyards, mines and factories, were now looking for higher wages to cope with inflation. Meanwhile those who had fought the good fight in Flanders or France were now looking for jobs and other forms of compensation, such as housing assistance and back pay due to them.

General dissatisfaction led to more strikes, and more serious strikes. These days, anywhere there was industry there was an element of industrial strife.

These problems aside, the first twenty years of the new century were positive in many respects. It was a period of great social improvement; legislation was passed raising the minimum age for child employment; limiting hours of work for women; and mandatory schooling. For the first time governments at all levels began to take their responsibilities seriously in the public health field, and steps were taken to fight these problems. It was none too soon.

Poverty, poor working conditions, and overcrowding in the cities had created public health hazards not met before. Tuberculosis was claiming thousands of lives every year; venereal diseases were rampant; an epidemic of Spanish 'Flu took a heavy toll. Another concern was the perennially high rate of alcoholism, with its collateral concerns of violence and absenteeism. In 1917, Walter Foster's otherwise liberal government, introduced legislation governing the licensing of all liquor sales outlets, and opted for total prohibition two years later — with all the predictable results.

On a more positive note, women were allowed to vote in provincial elections at last. It had been a long and frustrating battle, and it would be a few years yet before women were allowed to run for the offices they were voting for. And... for perhaps the first time — but certainly not the last — voices were raised against the widespread practices of political patronage and corruption.

Fifteen

❦

Deep Depression
1920-1940

The upsurge in business that accompanied The Great War, as it was known at the time, did not keep going much past Armistice Day; by 1920 the region was back into recession. The "boom or bust" cycle that New Brunswickers were becoming increasingly familiar with, would now throw them into a long period of considerably more bust than boom. In the face of more competition from abroad and elsewhere in Canada, regional businesses — now controlled by outside interests — retrenched.

During this period farming underwent some radical changes. In the atmosphere of an evolutionary, survival of the fittest world, the more efficient farmers survived — even thrived — while others failed. Farms became fewer but bigger as progressive, business minded operators took land over from their more casual neighbours.

This factor changed the whole complexion of rural life in the province, not just the number and size of farms being worked. Fewer, more efficient farms meant fewer farm hands, and those who had to leave agricultural life had to either move to the city to seek work, or look for part-time work in the woods or the fishery, While agriculture was undergoing its changes, much the same sort of face lifting was taking place in the fishery. Much like farming, the fishery, for the most part, consisted of individuals and their immediate kinsfolk, working as family units, perhaps with the odd hired hand.

The threat faced by these fishermen came from the increased use of steam trawlers. These larger, more efficient crafts sailing farther and faster, easily out produced the inshore fisherman, resulting in lower prices and more centralized processing plants. The inshore men countered with a remarkably well organized co-operative movement which helped them greatly, but the scene was set for the systematic rape of the Eastern Seabord's ocean fishery.

Changes had likewise taken place in the forestry industry. For all the previously stated reasons, lumbering was in decline. There were still plenty of sawmills about, but in terms of economic importance they were now secondary to the pulp and paper industry. A mill was built in Bathurst; the Frasers built another near Newcastle; and further mills were opened in Dalhousie and Saint John.

These mills were able to use the smaller softwood that was of no use to the sawmills, and supplies of material were plentiful. However the huge capital sums required to set up these pulp mills, demanded financial resources far beyond those available locally; and local ownership of industry continued to erode. Outside money flooded in, and the resource was removed from the province — along with the profits. More rural workers moved to the towns.

Labour unrest that had characterized the industrial scene before the Great War, returned with a vengeance in the twenties. Faced with stiffer competition in the lagging post-war economy, employers tried to roll back the wage gains that labour had made, while labour tried just as hard to hang on to any ground they had made.

Jam of Ernest Hutchinson's logs. *Courtesy: PANB #P6-197*

The impersonality of Big Business and Big Labour forged the system of confrontational relations, still hanging like a sullen weight around the necks of labour/management relations today. Strikes became more frequent and more bitter.

New Brunswick's eight year fiasco with Prohibition was responsible for creating one of the region's few growth industries for the period: rum running. Many of the fishermen were quick to discover that life was easier and more profitable, ferrying alcohol from St. Pierre and Miquelon, the wide open French colony off Newfoundland's south coast, to the parched populations of New England and the Maritimes.

Profits were good, and the chances of being caught very small. A long rugged coastline made effective policing almost impossible, so when it dawned on the province that they never had a prayer of imposing their own brand of sanctity upon their ungrateful subjects, Prohibition was repealed in 1927. They realized that they had been missing out on the world's steadiest source of income and took over the liquor trade, which they have been running profitably ever since.

After Wall Street crashed in 1929, the cycle of world trade took a universal nose dive; for all the usual reasons New Brunswickers felt the effects, a little harder, and a little faster than most. At the opening of the decade there had been scope for optimism. The pulp and paper industry continued its expansion with new mills opening, and existing mills being expanded. The Port of Saint John, one of the main exits and entry points for Canadian trade while the St. Lawrence was frozen shut, continued to be upgraded with Canadian funds.

Optimism soon turned to despair as little understood economic forces plunged the economy into a downturn, deeper and more devastating than ever before. Unemployment reached 19% in New Brunswick in the 1930s, and there were few of the social underpinnings that exist today. Heavy provincial debt loads left few dollars available for the subsistence of a constituency struck with mass unemployment. The ball got tossed back and forth between the three levels of government, In the end much of the burden fell upon the shoulders of the municipal authorities, and with such disparity in the relative prosperity of one municipality over the next, the obvious result was a huge disparity in relief payments.

The Great Depression broke another pattern. Since the whole continent was severely affected, the option of outmigration was closed to the unemployed. The United States closed its borders, and authorities across the Dominion closed their books to all outsiders.

Out of all the make-work projects, designed to ease the pressure of unemployment in this era, the most imaginative was a 'back to the land' program. The province opened up new lands, and abandoned farmland, offering them as grants to those who were up to the challenge. A number of these new areas were initiated, particularly in the north, since the idea seemed to have a particular appeal to the Acadians. Life was hard for these twentieth century settlers since the new communities had few if any of the facilities that they were used to — schools for instance. Life was not made any easier, by virtue of the fact that the land had to be cleared manually, since few Acadians could afford to equip themselves with the necessary machinery. The scheme was a long way short of an unqualified success, but at worst opened up new areas, and resulted in a great deal of roadbuilding.

Clustered in the impoverished north and eastern counties the Acadians were particularly hard hit by the depression, many of them coming close to starvation. Nevertheless the time became for them an era of relatively high activism. The question of language instruction in schools had always been a bone of contention, since the Acadian children were forced to learn English in the early grades at the same time they were trying to absorb the general curriculum. The results had been academically disappointing and the dropout problem epidemic; over half the students would be gone by Grade Five.

With a rapidly growing sense of identity, and a strong suspicion that English-speaking New Brunswickers were less likely to be laid off in a dwindling economy, the Acadians demanded the right to be served in their own language — a demand that was to have far-reaching effects down the road. The Roman Catholic Church also made a significant move — recognizing the special religious needs of the Acadians. The Church, for the first time, appointed a French-speaking Bishop of Moncton. Up to this point most had come under the fold of the Bishop of Chatham — who would normally be of Irish descent.

The depression years were a hard testing ground for organized labour. There was a tendency for employers to take advantage of high unemployment rates by lowering wages, and taking every opportunity to replace union with non-union workers, ready to work at any price. Concerned by an apparent flourishing of Communism among organized labour, organized religion under the leadership of the Roman Catholic Church strongly endorsed the Co-operative movement.

Sixteen

❖

War and Alphabet Soup
1940-1960

In the autumn of 1939 global conflict came to the aid of the economy once more. No sooner had Britain declared war on Germany than Canada followed suit days later on September 10th. After a period of several months during which Britain and France glared at Germany over their impregnable defenses, the Germans swept around them. France collapsed just six weeks after the opening offensive, leaving the British Army backed up against the Straits of Dover at Dunkirk. Canada was left as Britain's most powerful ally. As the British fought tooth and nail to stave off threatened invasion in the Battle of Britain, Canadian airmen flocked to the island's defense.

Perhaps because the threat from World War 11 was more immediate, enlistment in New Brunswick was considerably brisker than it had been in 1914. Almost half the eligible men volunteered. War came right to the doorstop on the East Coast in the form of U-boat wolf packs stalking the seas around the Atlantic Provinces for naval or merchant shipping.

The economy suddenly accelerated from slow to top speed; where men had vainly been looking for work, work was now looking for men. Since the Maritimes would probably become the front line against Hitler, in the event of Britain's fall, there was an urgent need for a build-up of military bases.

Along with other major Atlantic ports, Saint John was outfitted with anti submarine defenses, against the threat of invasion; the R.C.A.F. built airbases at Chatham and Saint John; training schools for airmen from all over the British Commonwealth were established at Pennfield and Stanley; army bases were set up at Edmundston and Sussex; and there was a prisoner of war camp at Ripples.

An important step for Saint John's future was the development of the dry-dock at the Saint John Shipyard. The yard received some benefit from the shipbuilding boom enjoyed by many centres but gained enormous amounts of work repairing ships that plied the Atlantic carrying vital supplies and war material for Britain. In the port, longshoremen worked around the clock, moving the goods through that Britain needed for its survival.

New Brunswickers fought or served in all branches of the armed services but three units had a particularly New Brunswick flavour.

The Carleton and York Regiment of infantry had its roots in two militia units dating back to 1787, and could include in their battle honours South Africa, and many of the great battles of the First World War: The Somme, Vimy, Passchendaele, Arras in 1917 and 1918, and the Hindenberg Line. This war would find them in the unsung but brutally hard fighting that gradually pushed an incredibly stubborn German army out of Sicily and up through the mountains of Italy. This campaign did not get all the press that D Day and the Invasion of Normandy received, but D Day could not have happened had not so many of Hitler's troops been diverted to repel the invasion from the south. The regiment took part in the landings on Sicily and Reggio on the mainland. They fought through Ortona; The Gully; and the Liri Valley; they were in on the three major battles of the campaign for the Hitler and Gothic Lines; the Rimini Line; and the Romagna. After engaging the Germans on the Winter Line in Northern Italy the regiment was diverted to the Battle in Holland, where fanatical Nazis were making their last desperate stand to keep allied troops out of the Fatherland. Their casualty figures indicate the kind of fighting they were exposed to — 324 killed, 1033 wounded.

Alongside the Carleton and Yorks in the Italian Campaign were the 8th Canadian Hussars, with their home base in Sussex, Kings County. They fought in this war as the 5th Canadian Armoured Regiment. Like their fellow New Brunswickers they were also diverted to Holland in April, 1945. There was some political pressure for the British to beef up the Empire's presence on the Western Front where they were by now heavily outnumbered by the Americans. The job in Italy was essentially done, so many of the Commonwealth troops were therefore diverted to Northern Europe. These two New Brunswick regiments were among them.

Like the Carleton and Yorks, The North Shore (New Brunswick) Regiment was an infantry unit with its roots far back in the county militias, in this case the militias of the counties of Northumberland, Gloucester, and Restigouche. They too carried battle honours from the First World War: Arras, 1917 and 1918, Hill 70, Ypres, Amiens, and the Hindenberg Line. Unlike their brother regiment, they were involved in the Normandy landings, storming the beach at St. Aubin sur Mer on June 6th, 1944. The regiment was involved in the heavy fighting around Caen, Carpiquet, Brettville sur Odon, and Quesnay Wood, eventually joining their fellow New Brunswickers in the fight for the liberation of Holland where they saw action on the Polders and at Zutfen. Considering their relatively short time at the front, their casualty figures were appalling — 370 killed, 926 wounded.

Once the war was over, all the old problems returned, as if they had never left. The prosperity brought by the war years, had been mainly due to federal expenditures on wartime projects: war-related shipbuilding; the huge amount of traffic through the port; and construction of military bases. Manufacturing was still — perhaps even more — concentrated in the interior of the country, and many of these plants were easily switched to peacetime production, while activity in the Maritimes languished.

The attitude of the Federal Government to repeated pleas from the Atlantic Region was, that due to a number of factors, concentration of industry in central Canada made more sense. Among the factors; distance from markets; lack of hydro-electric facilities; and skilled labour. It was the classic 'chicken and egg' theme. Markets are where one finds them — New England is on the doorstep. When Premier J.B.McNair approached Ottawa for assistance in funding hydro-electric energy, he was refused. Skilled labour will not stay where skilled labour is not needed.

However, there were a few bright spots. In the post-war period's attempt to foster secondary industry; Fraser Companies of Edmundston built a second, smaller mill on the Miramichi, above Newcastle, and K.C.Irving bought and modernized a mill at the Reversing Falls in Saint John. Irving was already well established as a force in the region's petroleum industry, and was well on his way to creating an industrial group that would dominate the Atlantic economy in years to come.

Born in Buctouche of Presbyterian Scots ancestry, Kenneth Colin Irving and his three sons were undeterred by distance from markets. Eventually supertankers from around the world would bring crude oil to the Irving deep water facility at Mispec near Saint John; which would be pumped to the Irving Oil refinery in East Saint John, refined and transported by Irving trucks or Irving ships to destinations in Eastern Canada and the Northeastern United States; to be sold as refined product in over three thousand Irving service stations.

The family would come to be one of the most extensive landowners in neighbouring Maine with their giant forest interests. Irving newsprint would penetrate markets in the United States and Europe. Their interests would broaden into agriculture and merchandising; into so many spheres, in fact that it would sometimes be hard to find a business that they were not involved in. It would be through the Irving family that shipbuilding would return to Saint John in a major way, when they purchased the dry dock in Courtenay Bay, from C.N.Wilson.

K.C.Irving was not the first industrialist to be fathered by New Brunswick. There were a pair of notables from the north of the province — Max Aitken and James Dunn — but Irving stayed in his native province to make his fortune; it would be a fortune on a world class scale.

James Dunn, or Sir James Dunn as he finished life, started life in Bathurst in 1874 and was educated in the Bathurst school system. He took his law degree at Dalhousie University in Halifax and was called to the bar in Nova Scotia, Quebec and the Northwest Territories. Despite his legal background he seemed to find the world of business more compelling, and by the age of twenty-seven he was a member of the Montreal Stock Exchange, at that time the premier stock exchange in Canada. Five years later found him in London creating the merchant banking firm of Dunn Fisher and Co. By 1935 he was President and Chairman of the Board of the giant Algoma Steel. Sir James married three times, his last bride being his former private secretary Anastasia Marcia Christoforides. He died in 1956 at St. Andrews N.B., leaving an estate of $70,000,000.

Although James Dunn and Max Aitken came from the same part of the world and were always the best of friends, they were a long way from being peas from the same pod. An indifferent student, Max struggled through the Newcastle school system and failed in his attempt to enter law school. One of nine children, he must have been something of a trial to his rather strait-laced parents. The father himself was a man of learning, university educated and a lifelong scholar, who might have expected better marks, but his marks matched his bad behaviour. Nevertheless any attempt that he made in entrepreneurial schemes were always highly successful — from selling eggs at the age of eight, to founding Royal Securities in his twenties. In 1907 he moved to Montreal, Canada's commercial center, and bought control of Montreal Trust. He organized a number of cement firms into the Canada Cement Company, and likewise a number of steel mills into The Steel Company of Canada, to combat the huge conglomerates that were flourishing in the United States.

By 1910 Aitken was establishing himself in London, at that time the center of the greatest empire the world had ever seen. He took to London like a rabbit takes to procreation, using his great personal charm to advantage in forging ties with the rich and powerful — including John Buchan — later to be the Governor General of Canada, and Andrew Bonar Law, a fellow New Brunswicker from Rexton. Law would become Prime Minister of Great Britain until forced to retire from sickness. It was Andrew Bonar Law who encouraged Aitken to run for parliament. A major factor in his election was his wife Gladys, a tireless worker and by his own admission a much better speaker than he. Never one to insist upon starting at the bottom he was happy to accept a knighthood from George V during his first year in politics. Meanwhile his Canadian and British business interests were booming.

When the First World War broke out it was a given fact that Canada, as a member of the Empire, would come to Britain's aid; but this time it would be on a different basis than before. The British assumed that Canadian troops would be sent over to be used as reinforcements for the British Army. This was not at all what Ottawa wanted and Max Aitken had the political clout to insist that the Canadians would come to fight, but as Canadian units with Canadian officers.

Max Aitken's first venture into journalism came in the First War as he sought out facts of Canada's participation and reported their doings to an eager audience at home. As if sealing his destiny to a life in journalism, his friends in government had him appointed Minister of Information. It was as a result of his efforts in the war that he was awarded the title of Lord Beaverbrook, after the name of a small stream he had fished as a boy.

With his friend Andrew Bonar Law falling to sickness, and a subsequent change of government, he left government and devoted his energies to the rescue of *The Daily Express* which in time would be the flagship of his newspaper chain. His knack for picking the right friends did not let him down. R.B.Bennett, an old friend from Chatham N.B. just down river from Newcastle, was now Prime Minister of Canada. He also became close with a rising figure in the British Conservative Party by the name of Winston S. Churchill.

After the outbreak of the Second World War, and the near disaster of Dunkirk; Churchill, now in power, quickly grasped the fact that the only thing that could save Britain from defeat would be the Royal Air Force. He sent for 'The Beaver' and gave him one task: the buildup of the air force. At the time the R.A.F.'s fighters were outnumbered three to one by the Luftwaffe and the outlook could not have been more bleak. He cracked the whip and as a result of his phenomenal energy production went from 183 planes per month to 471. Those numbers were sustained above the level of the losses which were also phenomenal. Even the Archtyrant Josef Stalin was not immune from the Beaver's charm; he was one of very few people from the West — from anywhere — that he trusted.

At the age of eighty-four, and for many years a widower, he married his old friend's widow — Lady Dunn, 'Christofor', but he was to die the following year. Although he spent much of his life away from the province of his birth the Beaver kept close ties. As Chancellor of the University of New Brunswick he was no figurehead but took a close interest in university affairs. He used his great wealth to give U.N.B. many scholarships and facilities. He remembered his old friends and fellow New Brunswickers Bennett and Bonar Law with the donation of a library. The City of Fredericton was presented with an art museum together with a remarkable collection. Naturally his hometown in the Miramichi was not forgotten, both Newcastle and Chatham receiving many facilities.

The Irvings were joined by another family whose business, though more specialized, would also spread throughout the world. The McCains operating out of a tiny Upper St. John Valley community called Florenceville, starting as potato growers, would develop into one of the world's leading frozen food processors.

The first McCains had come to Florenceville by way of Quebec City, from Donegal in 1820. The family set themselves up as farmers and businessmen, and by the 1930s and 1940s Andrew McCain was exporting seed potatoes. On his death bed he gathered his sons about him and gave them a final word of advice. "If you ever have a problem and don't know which way to turn, go down the road and ask old man MacIsaac — whatever he says, do the opposite." They never looked back.

Notwithstanding the bright spots, in the late 40s and early 50s New Brunswick was verging on bankruptcy and there was little relief in sight. The familiar cycle of outmigration of people and capital resumed its debilitating tread.

By the time the province shifted uneasily into the fifties, even the Federal Government found it glaringly apparent that there were very serious problems in Atlantic Canada. In 1949 Newfoundland had joined confederation with her own litany of crises and complaints, and it was clear that the whole region would have to join forces to make their point in Ottawa. Thus the first of an alphabet soup of organizations was born.

The Atlantic Provinces Economic Council (A.P.E.C.) was formed to make an in-depth study of the region's economic needs and strengths; and to inject some measure of co-ordination in trying to meet these goals. A.P.E.C. would be followed by A.R.D.A., D.R.E.E., A.C.O.A. and so on.

At the same time studies conducted by the Federal Government, convinced the bureaucrats of something they should have known all along; allowing the whole East Coast to drift into an economic disaster zone, was not necessarily going to be of any benefit to Central Canada. This time when Ottawa was bombarded by grievances from the whole Atlantic Region they got the point and started to listen.

In the meantime the mammoth St. Lawrence Seaway project had gone through, siphoning yet more traffic away from East Coast ports. This loss was compounded by Ottawa going to considerable expense employing ice-breakers to keep the Seaway open far beyond the normal shipping season. Port traffic in Saint John dwindled to the point where the port was little more than a last resort for winter shipping.

Ottawa finally bent under pleas from Premier Hugh John Flemming and agreed to share some of the costs of the Beechwood Hydro-Electric Dam. The wisdom of damming one of the world's great salmon rivers is another issue: they would do it bigger and better at Mactaquac twelve years later in 1967.

Seventeen

⌘

The Long Climb Back
1960-?

It seems, in retrospect, that the province's economic fortunes had hit an all time low in the late forties and early fifties, and was now starting the long climb back to its rightful position in Canadian society. All the basics were there, abundant natural resources, a sturdy resilient people, and a province of remarkable natural beauty.

New Brunswick was slow to take advantage of its natural attributes, and for years served as a corridor to Nova Scotia and Prince Edward Island, who marketed their wares much more aggressively. Saint John, justly proud of its Loyalist background, heavily promoted its points of historical interest, but gave barely a thought to a breathtaking coastline, and perhaps the most beautiful river system in the world.

The construction of King's Landing on the Mactaquac headpond, and the Acadian Village near Caraquet, were steps in the right direction; as were the National Parks at Alma on the Bay of Fundy, and Kouchibouguac on the warm waters of Northumberland Strait. Tourism become a major industry and has scope to grow much more.

During the sixties there seemed to be an air of renewed optimism around the province, at times verging on the visionary.

There was fresh interest in harnessing Fundy's gigantic tides — up to fifty feet in places — for hydro- electricity, and a great deal of thought was given to three very big projects that came to be known as 'the three Cs'.

The Chignecto Canal, as the term suggests, called for a fifteen mile canal across the Chignecto isthmus giving shipping from northern Europe or the St. Lawrence, more direct access to the Port of Saint John. K.C.Irving was one of the most vocal supporters of this plan, but since Saint John's gain would be Halifax's loss, Nova Scotia was cool to the idea. It was an interesting project, one that probably would have benefited Saint John, especially Irving interests, but it was not to happen.

The Corridor Road, running from the Trans Canada Highway at Fredericton to Montreal, was to cut across northern Maine, by way of Bangor and Sherbrooke, Quebec, in an almost straight line. This route would have cut about two hundred miles (320 km) off the trip from industrial Saint John to Montreal and Toronto, giving considerable savings for truckers, but it was not to be, either.

The Causeway from Cape Tormentine to Borden, Prince Edward Island — one of the fixed link options, along with a bridge and a tunnel (or any combination thereof) — returned like a stubborn furball in the Federal throat. Of the three potential projects this would be the only one to bear fruit — in the form of a bridge — and it would take another forty years to ripen.

The fixed link from New Brunswick to Prince Edward Island – christened, to no one's great surprise, the Confederation Bridge – opened amid much fanfare, and ahead of schedule in the summer of 1997. It should be said that most of the fanfare took place at the Island end of the bridge, since the New Brunswick government were more than a little sour at the minimal amount of economic benefit that had come the province's way during the bridge's construction. It had always been considered an Island project and this premise was exercised to the point of being whimsical. All the population of Prince Edward Island may not have been in favour of the bridge; feeling that the distinctive character of the province would be ruined by the fixed link, but that did not stop everyone from using it. The Island has been enjoying a much improved tourist trade since the opening. The only sour note is the frequency that large unladen trucks have been kept off the bridge due to high winds, causing long delays.

The Acadians, who were still lagging far behind the rest of the population in terms of living standards, education and employment opportunities, made great strides in the sixties. The University of Moncton was established to act as an educational centre for the regions' Acadians; and social legislation effected significant changes in the whole social background of the province.

In June 1960 voters overwhelmingly elected a Liberal government under the leadership of Louis J. Robichaud an aggressive young Acadian lawyer, and a remarkable politician. 'Little Louis' was not the first Acadian to be premier of the province. Peter 'Good Roads' Veniot had held the post from 1923 to 1925, but he was the first to be elected. Determined to do something about the inequities that existed throughout New Brunswick society, he set up a program under the label of Equal Opportunity.

Under Equal Opportunity, the old county councils were abolished and replaced by locally elected councils in the individual towns and villages; areas that were not in either category were placed under direct provincial supervision. Saint John, which had been flanked by the City of Lancaster on the west and the Parish of Simonds on the east was expanded to encompass the outlying districts, with a view to streamlining services.

Under this ambitious plan the one-room schoolhouses that had dotted the countryside disappeared, to be replaced by large centralized complexes with infinitely better facilities, and higher teaching standards. Education, Public Health, Social Welfare, and Justice were all taken under the wing of the provincial government.

These measures were not geared to target the Acadians in particular; they were directed towards levelling the harsh disparities that existed between municipalities of varying economic health. Nor did they meet with everyone's approval. The plan was greeted with much reservation in the more highly developed southern region, because it meant that for a while the lion's share of funds available for schools and hospitals would be diverted elsewhere. The opposition was vocal but the same arguments that applied to Maritime development as a viable part of Canada, applied to the development of the north and eastern parts of the province. Enough people thought so to keep Robichaud in power for ten years. Only two of his predecessors had lasted longer.

The Sixties were also a time of heightened racial tensions. The Federal Government's legislation giving French an equal footing with English was adopted by New Brunswick, making it the first and only officially bilingual province in Canada. Equal Opportunity; continuous friction between Ottawa and Quebec; the Official Languages Act; and increased militancy among Acadians, all conspired to make the English speakers feel picked upon. There were charges of reverse discrimination as more and more Civil Service positions were made available to Acadians.

Of course it was the age of dissent everywhere, and racial tensions were not restricted to the English and the French. Native and black groups became more aggressive in pressing for their right to a share in society, mirroring movements elsewhere, particularly in the United States.

When Louis Robichaud went down to defeat in 1970 at the hands of Conservative Richard Hatfield, there was concern among the Acadians that the progress that they were making would come to a grinding halt, or even an about turn under an administration that had only two Acadians in its caucus. In fact Hatfield turned out to be one of the best friends that they ever had, and it was to a great extent the Acadian vote that would keep him in power until 1987.

By now Governments at all levels were concentrating on industrial development and wherever government funds abound so do the flimflam artists. The most memorable of the species to invade New Brunswick was Malcolm Bricklin, an enterprising young man with cowboy boots, photo-sensitive shades, and the vision of a sports car. He found a receptive ear in Richard Hatfield, who found space for him in Saint John and Minto, and nine million dollars in funding. Malcolm must have had trouble believing his luck. Having installed most of his immediate family in positions of importance in the company, he imported a number of executives from Detroit, and set about building his dream car. It was a sporty looking rig distinguished by unusual colours, unusual contours, and an even more unusual system for doors. When in the open position, these strongly resembled gull's wings, appropriate enough, given the obvious parallels between that bird's insatiable appetite, and Bricklin's ability to absorb government funds. Every

Friday relatives and Detroit executives alike could be seen elbowing their way to the airport's departure counter, to pick up their company-paid tickets home for the week-end. By the fall of 1975, just over two years after the joyful announcement, twenty million dollars had evaporated along with any hope of success.

It would not be fair to characterize Hatfield's reign by failed investments. New Brunswick's industrial base continued to expand. The Port of Saint John underwent a major development with a new container terminal, a highly successful forest products terminal, and a terminal to handle the output of the new potash mines around Sussex. Social conditions also continued to improve and racial tensions between the two main ethnic groups abated. However, like so many politicians, Hatfield was unable or unwilling to read writing on walls. Latent concerns over his lifestyle were hardly put to rest when R.C.M.P. officers discovered a small stash of marijuana in his baggage on the royal plane during a visit by Queen Elizabeth. Questions about Hatfield's ability to lead his party, and a stubborn refusal to step down, led to the most catastrophic defeat in Canadian political history. In 1987 Frank McKenna's Liberals counted 58 seats to the Conservatives 0.

A decade later the Tories were still in disarray, factionalised by the emergence of the right wing Confederation of Regions party and seemingly endless infighting over leadership. In an age of ruthless belt tightening the Liberals, under McKenna were able to be as ruthless as anybody, without seeming to lose public support. Frank McKenna, an energetic young lawyer from the Miramichi, was one of the stars among the provincial premiers and worked tirelessly to bring jobs to New Brunswick, and much to the annoyance of some of his fellow premiers, was not above raiding other provinces to that end. New Brunswick was one of the first provinces to be able to put its millstone of a deficit in order.

When McKenna surprised a lot of people by fulfilling a decade old promise to retire after ten years in office, the mantle was passed on to Camille Theriault a career politician with strong roots in the Acadian part of the province. In early 1999, in order to consolidate his position and to ensure that his liberals would carry through another term in government, Theriault called a spring election. He shouldn't have. The Conservatives had finally got their house in order, and mastered the concept of making strides without stumbling over their own feet. Splinter groups had dissipated, and under the leadership of a youthful Bernard Lord trounced a shell shocked government, leaving them with a lowly ten seats. Once again the New Brunswick voters proved that they should never be taken for granted.

The fact that the federal Progressive Conservative Party lost the federal election in 1993 surprised no one. It was the scope of the loss that was so astonishing. In the entire country only two PCs were returned - the popular, young Jean Charest from Quebec, and the ex-mayor of Saint John, Elsie Wayne. So from 1993 to 1997 most of the City of Saint John and surrounding area could claim to be on a first name basis with the deputy leader of the PC Party, also with fifty percent of the Tory caucus. Her career has been a remarkable achievement for a woman who had not even entered politics until her mid-forties.

Her political life started as an activist in her home neighbourhood of Glen Falls - part of the area once occupied by the Great Marsh of East Saint John - which was subject to frequent flooding. Her efforts to bring attention to the problem led first to a seat on City Council, and from there to the Mayoralty. From there the move to federal politics was as smooth and natural as all her previous progressions. She had been Saint John's first woman mayor, and was succeeded by another – Shirley McAlary, now in *her* second term.

In another breakthrough by women, Margaret Norrie McCain related by marriage to the McCains of Florenceville, breathed fresh air into the position of Lieutenant Governor. From June 1994 to April 1977 she held the post with great sensitivity and charm. Margaret McCain was an activist Lieutenant Governor, taking an active interest in the field of family violence, and the care of battered women. Her husband, Wallace McCain, had fallen out with his brother Harrison and had left the family firm to take over Maple Leaf Foods Inc. which had made it necessary for him to move to Toronto. Eventually she felt she had to retire from the position to rejoin her family there. She, too was replaced on her retirement by Marilyn Trenholme Counsell, a New Democrat, who proved the fact by promptly sending the limo provided back to the dealer.

As the twentieth century draws to an end, New Brunswickers can look back at the various fortunes — good or ill — that history has brought them and be forced to wonder what the future might bring. One hundred years ago the shipbuilding trade was in a state of total collapse. The forests had been stripped of much of their wealth. The steam engine had brought mobility and with it, access to new markets. The same invention also powered an infinitely more efficient fishing fleet — so much so that the fish stock has been brought to a crisis level. The two dozen, or so, railway lines that crisscrossed the province at the turn of the century have been reduced to two lines operating four tracks. (One is forced to wonder how much longer it will be before CN will rationalize the closing of one of their two lines that run across the province from northwest to southeast.)

In 1983 shipbuilding returned to Saint John with a vengeance when the Irving owned Saint John Shipbuilding Ltd. was successful in securing a contract to build twelve ships for the Canadian Patrol Frigate Program. Nine of these ships were built in Saint John while the remaining three were built by a subcontractor in Quebec under Irving's management. The last ship was handed over to the Royal Canadian Navy in July 1996; the overall contract having been fixed at $6.2 billion.

The environmental damage done in the past cannot be undone. Only in the forests of the Christmas Mountains can trees still be found that can remind us what our forests used to look like. For that reason, if for no other, the forestry industry will have to cut them down — they stand as a living rebuke to man's stupidity.

Will the damage be allowed to continue? Signs for the future are mixed. Efforts toward reforestation tend to take the form of 'orchards' of fast-growing species yielding high in pulp. These groves lacking any form of diversity create near ecological vacuums — nobody is planting hardwoods. The recent shift to hardwoods for pulp production is frightening. What will become of our hardwood stands?

The population base of the province is stable, but the unemployment rate swings with the ebb and flow of world economics, apparently unaffected by political involvement.

One of the most technologically advanced telephone systems anywhere has made New Brunswick a haven for companies involved with 'call centres' and telemarketing. Someone in New Mexico needing service for a copying machine might have to make the arrangement through someone in New Brunswick — that is the way the world runs today.

New Brunswickers, particularly the Acadians, watch events in Quebec with apprehension as, once again, threats of separation echo around 'la belle province.' New Brunswick would be affected more drastically than most. Along with the rest of

Atlantic Canada the province would be geographically severed from the remainder of the country. The Acadians fear that political separation from Quebec might endanger their hard-won cultural rights.

All problems and potential problems notwithstanding, New Brunswickers can take comfort in the knowledge that communication will make outmigration unnecessary for many people; indeed many may come to New Brunswick in search of a quality of life that is not accessible to them in the more heavily populated centres of the country. Who knows?

Notes

One/The First Nations

1. Trueman, Stuart. 1966. *The Ordeal of John Gyles, Being an Account of His Odd Adventures, Strange Deliverances, etc., as a Slave of the Malicetes.* Toronto: McClelland & Stewart.

Two/The First Settlers

1. Trueman, Stuart. 1966. *The Ordeal of John Gyles, Being an Account of His Odd Adventures, Strange Deliverances, etc., as a Slave of the Malicetes.* Toronto: McClelland & Stewart.

Four/The Expulsion of the Acadians

1. Ross, Sally and Deveau, Alphonse. 1992. *The Acadians Past & Present.* Halifax: Nimbus Publishing.

Ten/The Irish

1. O'Driscoll, Robert and Reynolds, Lorna. (Eds.) 1988. *The Untold Story: The Irish in Canada.* Toronto: Celtic Arts of Canada.

2. *Ibid.*

Maps

The historical maps of Saint John and Passamaquoddy Bay are based on maps from W.F. Ganong's *Historic Sites of New Brunswick.*

Bibliography

Call, Frank Oliver. 1930. *The Spell of Acadia*. Boston: L.C. Page & Co.

Carless, J.M.S. 1967. *The Union of the Canadas. The Growth of Canadian Institutions 1841-1857*. Toronto: McClelland & Stewart.

Clarke, George Frederick. 1970. *Someone Before Us. Our Maritime Indians*. Fredericton: Brunswick Press.

Condon, Anne Gorman. 1983. The Foundations of Loyalism. *The Loyal Americans*.

Driver, Harold E. 1969. *Indians of North America*. University of Chicago Press.

Ganong. W.R. Reprinted 1983. *Historic Sites in the Province of New Brunswick*. St. Stephen, NB: Print 'n Press.

Hamilton, W.D. 1987. *Miramichi Papers*. Fredericton: Micmac-Maliseet Institute, University of New Brunswick.

MacDonald, M.A. 1983. *Fortune and La Tour. The Civil War in Acadia*. Methuen Publications.

MacNutt, W.S. 1965. *The Atlantic Provinces. The Emergence of Colonial Society 1712-1857*. Toronto: McClelland & Stewart.

Maxwell, M.B. *History of Central New Brunswick*. Fredericton: Centennial Print & Litho Ltd.

Morton, Desmond. 1983. *A Short History of Canada*. Edmonton: Hurtig Publishers Ltd.

Nason, David. 1992. *Railways of New Brunswick*. Fredericton: New Ireland Press.

O'Driscoll, Robert and Reynolds, Lorna. (Eds.) 1988. *The Untold Story: The Irish in Canada*. Toronto: Celtic Arts of Canada.

Perley, Moses. *Camp of the Owls. Excerpts from Sporting Review 1836-1846*. London, England.

Ross, Sally and Deveau, Alphonse. 1992. *The Acadians Past & Present*. Halifax: Nimbus Publishing.

Trueman, Stuart. 1970. *An Intimate History of New Brunswick*. Toronto: McClelland & Stewart.

Trueman, Stuart. 1966. *The Ordeal of John Gyles, Being an Account of His Odd Adventures, Strange Deliverances, etc., as a Slave of the Malicetes*. Toronto: McClelland & Stewart.

Wright, Ester Clarke. 1949. *The St. John River*. Toronto: McClelland & Stewart.

Index

Index